The Magic Tanach
and Other Short Plays

Gabrielle Suzanne Kaplan

A.R.E. Publishing, Inc.
Denver, Colorado

Dedication
To my grandmother Minerva Bugen Auerbach, whose love both
of theater and of Judaism has deeply inspired my journey, and
to the blessed memory of my grandmother Beatrice Fisher
Kaplan, whose strong faith and commitment to Judaism
continue to guide me.

Acknowledgements
I wish to thank publishers Rabbi Raymond A. Zwerin and
Audrey Friedman Marcus of A.R.E. Publishing, Inc. for all of
their encouragement and support of my work. Also, much
gratitude goes to my parents and friends whose loving support
enabled me to create these plays.

Published by:
A.R.E. Publishing, Inc.
Denver, Colorado

Library of Congress Catalog Card Number 99-77394
ISBN 0-86705-044-6

Contents

• •

Introduction

My background as both a theater artist and a Religious School teacher has taught me that drama is a dynamic vehicle for understanding the Jewish experience. "Becoming" a character in and acting out our most sacred of stories allows us to know them on a level that is not always attained through other methodologies. It is empowering to play biblical characters, such as Moses and Miriam, historical characters, such as Maimonides and Golda Meir, or imaginary characters, such as those depicted in some of these plays, as they struggle with issues that resonate in the lives of today's students. Drama can lead to personal insight, can provoke discussion, and can open people to texts and to new ideas.

With this in mind, I have created this collection of 24 short plays for use in suppplementary and day schools, camps, youth groups, for retreats and synagogue programming. The subject matter includes Jewish holidays, wisdom literature, sacred texts, and Jewish values. Some plays are influenced by traditional sources, while others reflect traditional ideas in new ways. All of the plays lend themselves to discussion of Jewish issues, and are therefore suitable for teaching and reinforcing subjects taught in the classroom.

At the beginning of each play, there is a suggested age range. When choosing plays to read and/or perform, also keep in mind your curriculum and the abilities and interests of your students. All of the plays are relatively simple to stage. They can be performed as Readers Theater in the classroom, for other students, for shut-ins, and for parents. Or, they can be produced and performed more elaborately with costumes, props, and sets. Guidelines for these are suggested herein.

When using *The Magic Tanach and Other Short Plays* as a teaching tool, each player should have a copy of the book in order to assure a smooth reading. If a play is being used in a performance setting, it is proper to note the title of the play, the full name of the author, and the publisher of this book in the program.

May you and your students enjoy this opportunity to perform and to learn in a creative fashion!

The Sabbath Angels

(Grades 4-6)

Characters

Narrator
Mischievous Angel
Good Angel

Production Notes

This play serves as a good discussion on how we can best make Shabbat holy.

(Narrator stands in the middle of the angels.)

Narrator: Shalom, chaverim! Peace, friends. I am here today because I need your help . . . desperately! There is an argument going on, well not an argument exactly, more of say, a dispute. Yes, a dispute, no . . . not a dispute exactly. Perhaps we might call it a disagreement? Yes, that's it, a disagreement.

Mischievous Angel: Disagreement? It's a fight! A battle! A war!

Good Angel: Could we just talk this over, please? I'm sure we can reach an understanding . . .

Mischievous Angel: But you agreed! You agreed! You agreed!

Good Angel: Well, the first part sounded so good, I didn't realize . . .

Narrator: Excuse me, angels on high, I mean ministering angels, I mean . . .

Good Angel: I prefer Malachay HaShalom, angels of peace.

Mischievous Angel: Malachay HaSharayt, ministering angels, suits me fine.

1

Good Angel: Angels of peace has a good ring to it.

Mischievous Angel: Ministering angels is much better.

Good Angel: Angels of peace!

Mischievous Angel: Ministering angels!

Good Angel: Malachay HaShalom!

Mischievous Angel: Malachay HaSharayt!

Narrator: Angels, please stop! Our friends still don't know what the dilemma is!

Mischievous Angel: Well, that's easy — it goes like this. My pal and I here, we're angels.

Good Angel: That's malach in Hebrew. It means messenger. We are messenger from the Holy One, blessed be God.

Mischievous Angel: Excuse me, but would you let me finish telling the story?

Good Angel: Sorry, I was simply trying to clarify what the term angel means. It's not like we just fly around all day or sit on clouds. Being a messenger of the Holy One is not always easy work.

Mischievous Angel: That's one thing I'll agree with. Being an angel isn't exactly a picnic. But you gotta do your best to carry out the word . . .

Good Angel: Your best? Your best? (*Laughs hysterically.*) You must be joking! You couldn't mean that you, you mischievous angel, do your best — when you pulled that dirty trick on me . . .

Mischievous Angel: For crying out loud, that was no dirty trick, that was an honest to goodness deal.

Narrator: Angels! Angels! Please! I think I had better quickly summarize the story, with your approval, of course, because left to you our dear friends here, we may never find out exactly how . . .

Good Angel: That angel double-crossed me!

Mischievous Angel: DID NOT!

Good Angel: DID, TOO!

Narrator: Angels, angels, shame on you both! My dear friends, the story of this dispute, uh, disagreement, uh, conflict, according to the well-known teaching of Rabbi Yose ben Yehuda . . .

Good Angel: Who lived way back in the second century . . .

Narrator: Thank you, angel of peace, your knowledge is oh so helpful.

Mischievous Angel: Big whoop.

Narrator: Yes, Rabbi Yehuda's tale is a big whoop. According to him, two angels accompany a person home from the synagogue on the eve of every Shabbat.

Mischievous Angel: That's us!

Narrator: One is a good angel . . .

Good Angel: That's me!

Narrator: And one is, well, a not-so-good angel.

Mischievous Angel: I prefer the title "Mischievous Angel."

Narrator: Yes, Mischievous Angel, that will do. So, this Mischievous Angel . . .

Mischievous Angel: That's me!

3

Narrator: . . . made a deal with the Good Angel . . .

Good Angel: *C'est moi!*

Narrator: And the deal goes like this: when the angels look through the window of a Jewish home on Friday evening, and the family is celebrating Shabbat, you know, the candles are lit, a delicious meal is prepared, the parents and the children are happy just being together, then the Good Angel may say . . .

Good Angel: May it also be thus next Shabbat!

Narrator: And the not-so-good angel will say . . .

Mischievous Angel: Amen!

Good Angel: Oh, yes, yes, yes! I'll do it! That's a wonderful deal! Think of how we'll seal in Shabbat joy for so many families!

Mischievous Angel: But wait . . . there's more!

Narrator: The deal also works in reverse. That is, if these angels look in the window of the home, and the table isn't set, and no candles are lit, and the family, oh the poor family, is quarreling . . .

Good Angel: Not on Shabbat!

Narrator: Yes, dear angel, in some homes it is this way. And so our Mischievous Angel will say . . .

Mischievous Angel: May it also be thus next Shabbat!

Narrator: And you, Good Angel must say . . .

Good Angel: But I can't! I can't!

Mischievous Angel: Whispering willows, you already said yes to the deal! So now you need to seal my prayer.

4

Good Angel: I suppose a deal is a deal.

Narrator: Let's try this again. So, if a family isn't celebrating Shabbat, the Mischievous Angel says . . .

Mischievous Angel: May it also be thus next Shabbat

Narrator: Then the good angel must say . . .

Good Angel: Amen.

Narrator: Alas, now that you understand the situation, dear friends, tell me, how can we help to solve the problem this deal creates? How can we help people to celebrate Shabbat, the day of spiritual rest and renewal, if this Mischievous Angel has said such a sad prayer? Please, help me, friends. What can you and your family do to create a wonderful Shabbat? *(Takes audience suggestions.)* Those are wonderful ideas, friends. I am sure the Good Angel will be blessing you next week.

Good Angel: Amen!

Mischievous Angel: Hey, hey, hey, hey! Wait just a second, buddy! I don't appreciate you getting this whole group to gang up on me this way. Just cause I'm a little more mischievous than my awfully good friend here doesn't mean I don't deserve respect. After all, I am a malach, a messenger of the Holy One — so don't you think there may be a very good reason that I made that deal?

Good Angel: I never thought of that.

Narrator: Why I must say, neither did I. Do tell us, bad, I mean not-good, I mean, Mischievous Angel.

Mischievous Angel: Well, as we all know, observing Shabbat is a beautiful thing. But it's not always an easy thing. People are busy and they don't always want to take time out to thank the Holy One and count their blessings.

Good Angel: It makes me cry. People don't light Shabbat candles, or say Kiddush, or even sing Shabbat songs.

Mischevious Angel: My favorite is *"Shalom Alaychem."*

Good Angel: Mine, too.

Mischievous Angel: Hey, we agree on something! Anyway, the key to observing Shabbat, as I see it, is that you must want to do it. Not that somebody tells you you should or shouldn't, but that in your heart of hearts, you want to celebrate. You want to make Shabbat a special time to be with family and friends. But sometimes you only learn what your heart wants by struggling, by having obstacles to overcome. So if I see a family isn't celebrating and I say, "May it also be thus next Shabbat," then they have a stronger challenge to overcome.

Good Angel: And I have observed, in all my time as an angel, that sometimes people don't appreciate all the blessings they have until they've struggled with a big challenge.

Mischievous Angel: Look, I want people to have a beautiful Shabbat just as much you do. So I figure if they have week after week of fighting, and loneliness, and bad food . . .

Narrator: Bad food? Oh my!

Mischievous Angel: Then in the deepest part of their hearts, they'll realize that this is not the way the Holy One designed us to be.

Good Angel: I see your point. So tell me, friends, what will you and your family do this week to overcome this Mischievous Angel's challenge? *(Takes answers from audience again.)*

Narrator: Well, very good. All's well that ends well, as they say. And, my dear Mischievous Angel, I do apologize for, well for, being a bit, well just a tiny bit, biased . . .

Mischievous Angel: That's okay, buddy. I know what I'm doing. Remember, the very name of Israel means "God-wrestler." So I just help people get going with their wrestling match!

Good Angel: Yes, Jacob received the name Israel after he wrestled with an angel. And between you and me, my back is still sore from all that wrestling!

Mischievous Angel: That wasn't you wrestling Jacob!

Good Angel: Was too!

Mischievous Angel: WAS NOT!

Narrator: Oh, dear friends, I know time's up and you must be on your way. Thank you so much for helping me solve this problem. I hope each and every one of your Sabbaths will be more joyous than the last. And maybe next time I visit, you can help me solve . . .

Good Angel: Was too!

Mischievous Angel: Was not!

Narrator: . . . their next wrestling match.

The Cup, the Spice Box, and the Candle

●●●●●●●●●●●●●●●●●●●●●●●●●●●●●●●●●●●●●●

(Grades 1-3)

Characters

Spice box
Kiddush Cup
Havdalah Candle
Kids

Costumes

Simple signs or more elaborate creations can be used.

(Spice Box, Kiddush Cup, and Havdalah Candle stand center stage.)

Cup: Hey, wake up, candle! Wake up, spice box! The sun is almost setting.

Spice Box: Pardon me, but Havdalah does not begin until the sun is *absolutely* the whole way down and then some.

Candle: *(Yawning.)* Hey, she's right, you know. Havdalah doesn't begin until you can count three stars in the sky. And since it's still Shabbat, I'm enjoying the rest of my day of rest.

Cup: But we're in the middle of the city! Who can see stars? And, besides, I need someone to polish me. Since I'm a Kiddush Cup, they filled me with wine for Shabbat and I just don't feel ready for Havdalah without a good rubdown!

Spice Box: Oh, here, I'll do it. Well, I see the sun has set and Shabbat is over. We have Havdalah services for saying good-bye to Shabbat. Good-bye, Shabbat.

Candle: Boy, I really enjoyed my rest this Shabbat.

Cup: Me, too.

Spice Box: Me, too. Hey, Kiddush Cup, you look absolutely fabulous. Look at that sparkle! And I can see my sweet little spices reflecting off your side.

Candle: It's a good thing you're finished polishing . . . cause here they come!

Cup: And here you go! Pretty soon they're gonna light you.

Spice Box: Hey, candle, I was wondering why do you have so many wicks?

Candle: It's a tradition to use a candle with many wicks for Havdalah, as opposed to single wick candles for Shabbat. Havdalah marks the start of the work week, and fire is often a symbol of work.

Cup: Like for cooking, you need fire.

Spice Box: Or, like the metal workers who made me.

Candle: Exactly. Ohhh, listen, they're on their way in . . .

(Children enter, singing any song or niggun melody.)

Cup: Ohhh, that tickles, they've filled me with wine and are saying Kiddush.

Spice Box: That's a prayer to make the wine holy.

Cup: Well, they better not make any holey-s in me, or the wine will spill out!

Candle: Not full of holes, silly. Holy, you know, Kadosh.

Cup: Oh . . . Kadosh. Why didn't you say so?

Spice Box: Quiet, you two! Here's the big moment! Now everyone passes me around and takes a big sniff of my sweet smelling spices.

Candle: I was always kind of wondering, Spice Box, what exactly are you filled with?

Spice Box: Oh, anything sweet and delicious! Cinnamon, cloves, nutmeg, you name it. The idea is to remember how sweet Shabbat was and to carry that sweetness with you into the new week.

Cup: Hey, let me have a whiff. Mmmmm!

Candle: Oh, oh, oh, move over! It's my big moment! I'm hot stuff now!

Spice Box: What are they doing to you?

Candle: This ritual is very important, too. See, they're holding their hands in my candlelight to check them and see if they're ready to go back to work.

Cup: They also cast shadows on their palm and remember the difference between darkness and light.

Spice Box: Between rest and work.

Candle: Between the six days of work and Shabbat.

Cup: Okay, are you ready?

Candle: It can't be time! We just started.

Cup: Candle, remember, Havdalah is very important, but it's a short service!

Candle: Nothing else?

Spice Box: They said Kiddush, smelled my spices, and checked their fingers. I am absolutely sure it's over!

Candle: IF YOU SAY SO!

(Candle and Kiddush Cup bend and touch heads.)

Spice Box: Havdalah is over when the candle is put out in the remaining wine. Shavua Tov!

(Children sing "Eliahu Hanavi" and "Shavua Tov.")

Cup: Have a good week, everybody. I'm gonna rest up till next Shabbat.

Spice Box: Yes, that was exhausting. I think I'll just sit on this shelf for the next six days. How about you, candle?

Candle: Well, my cousin the birthday candle said he'd stop by later to visit, but I might take a little snooze till he comes. Shavua Tov — and get some sleep!

Cup: Nighty-night.

Spice Box: *(Falling asleep.)* A good week . . . a week of peace . . .

Rosh Chodesh: The New Moon

(Grades 7-12)

Cast of Characters

Mom
Dad
Danielle
Michael
Israelite Woman 1
Israelite Woman 2
Israelite Man 1
Israelite Man 2
Messenger
High Priest
Rabbi
Witness 1
Witness 2

Costumes and Props

Large costume jewelry is suitable for the Israelite Women and a bathrobe covered with gold foil will work nicely for the High Priest. Children have school books and Dad has a newspaper.

Setting

Minimal setting allows the characters to enter and exit easily. A few chairs and a table can serve as the family living room.

(Dad sits in chair reading a newspaper. Michael and Danielle are doing homework. Mom enters.)

Mom: Okay, Danielle, make sure to feed the cats. Michael, please put away the clean dishes. I guess that's it. I'll see you all later . . .

Danielle: Mom, where are you going?

Michael: You can't go out tonight. I need help with math!

Dad: Michael, I can help . . .

Michael: Well, but . . . it's just that Mom's a little better at fractions . . .

Mom: Your father can help tonight. I'm on my way to a Rosh Chodesh celebration.

Dad: It seems like you just went to one of those . . . last month.

Mom: Well, Rosh Chodesh is a celebration of the new moon . . . and we honor the moon every 29 or 30 days. In fact, the Jewish monthly calendar is based on the moon's cycle.

Danielle: Well, if it's a Jewish thing, why can't we all go?

Mom: My Rosh Chodesh group is made up of women only. Danielle, when you get older — or when you don't have so much homework — you can come with me.

Dad: Why is Rosh Chodesh such a women's thing?

Mom: Remember in Exodus when Moses goes up the mountain to get the Ten Commandments?

Michael: Yeah . . . and everyone freaks out and builds the golden calf.

Mom: Well, maybe not everybody . . .

(The Israelite people enter.)

Israelite Man 1: Great! Moses is gone, we're out here in the desert by ourselves, and we're supposed to pray to a God we can't even see. Yeah, right!

Israelite Woman 1: Moses will come back, he promised. Besides, remember when the Sea of Reeds parted? How could that have happened without God? I'm sure we'll be fine until Moses returns.

Israelite Man 1: You women are so naive! Well, I'm not waiting around. Let's make a god to protect us. Whaddya think?

Israelite Man 2: Sure, it's better than standing around. Let's make a calf. I've always liked calves. That'll protect us.

Israelite Woman 2: No way! I'm not making an idol.

Israelite Man 1: A golden calf . . . we'll need lots of gold, that's for sure! Hey, you ladies have all that nice gold jewelry on. Give it over and we'll melt it down!

Israelite Woman 1: This gold came with me as I danced across the Sea. There's no way I'll give it to you for your silly idol.

Israelite Woman 2: Me either! Come on, let's get the other women and we can sit together and pray until Moses gets back.

Israelite Man 2: Ahhh, forget the women! Let's go find some gold.

(They all exit.)

Mom: The Rabbis explained that because the women wouldn't help with making the golden calf, they were rewarded with a special holiday, Rosh Chodesh. Women didn't have to work when the new moon came.

Danielle: Wow! Those Israelite women were smart. Is that a true story?

Dad: It may or may not be true, but it does explain why Rosh Chodesh has been important to women for a long time.

Mom: Not just to women, though. Rosh Chodesh is mentioned in the Torah and all through the Hebrew Bible as a time for joy.

Michael: So all the people would celebrate the new moon. What if you lived where you couldn't see the moon — like in a city — where you usually can't even see stars.

Dad: Well, back then, people were mostly farmers or shepherds and there weren't skyscrapers to block your view . . . or smog or . . .

Danielle: I wished I lived back then.

(Witness 1, Witness 2, and High Priest enter.)

Witness 1: Hey! Yoo-hoo! Hey, anybody in the Temple?

High Priest: Just me, the High Priest. Can I help you?

Witness 2: Yeah, we were just wandering home through the fields, we're shepherds, see, and we were glancing up in the sky . . . You know how it's been dark the last couple of nights? Well, now we've got a new moon up there.

High Priest: Thanks for being the witnesses. A new moon is good news. It symbolizes that God is with us from month to month. Let me put on my special gold robe *(He does so.)* and I will announce the new moon! Then all of Israel can rejoice.

Witness 1: Sounds good to me! My family always has a special meal at the new moon. And, besides, I really wasn't in the mood to shear 207 sheep tomorrow.

High Priest: The moon never fails to have good timing.

Witness 2: You can say that again!

(They exit.)

Danielle: If Rosh Chodesh was such a big deal, why don't we make it a special day like we do Shabbat?

Mom: Good question. Rosh Chodesh never caught on like the other festivals. That's why many women's groups get together to celebrate the new moon. We believe that each month is a special gift. So why not celebrate?

Dad: Come to think of it, we do celebrate Rosh Chodesh at Shabbat services.

(Rabbi enters.)

Rabbi: May it be your will, our God, to renew us for this month, for goodness and for blessing. The beginning of the month of *[insert name of current month]* will fall on *[insert day of week]*. May this month bring goodness to us and to all of Israel.

(Rabbi exits.)

Michael: That's right. The Rabbi did announce the new month . . . just like the High Priest used to do.

Danielle: Mom, you're going to be late.

Mom: You're right, I should go. I'll see you all later!

(Mom exits.)

Dad: Chores. Homework. What do you think, kids?

Danielle: Well, it *is* a holiday.

Michael: I think kids and men should also celebrate Rosh Chodesh.

Dad: You're right. The work will wait. Let's go outside and look at the new moon!

(They exit.)

Wake Up!

(Grades 1-4)

Cast of Characters

Joey
Rachel
Dad
Peasant
Drummer
Townsperson 1
Townsperson 2
Child

Props

A cot or blankets and pillow to act as a bed
Percussion instruments (or a barrel or pot to bang on)
A wastebasket

Production Notes

This play, which introduces the idea of shofar and the concept of our ability to change, is appropriate for Rosh HaShanah or any time during the month of Elul.

(Joey is sleeping center stage. Rachel enters.)

Rachel: Joey! Wake up! It's time to get ready for services.

Joey: I don't want to get up! Let me sleep.

Rachel: But it's Rosh HaShanah, the birthday of the world! It's time to go to synagogue and see our friends!

Joey: You go . . . let me sleep.

Rachel: Don't you want to hear the shofar?

Joey: What's the big deal about the shofar? It's just a ram's horn.

Rachel: It's not just a ram's horn! It's special! We hear it every year on Rosh HaShanah and Yom Kippur.

Joey: But what can it *do*, Rachel? *Why* do we hear it on Rosh HaShanah? Oops, here comes Dad.

Dad: *(Entering.)* Are you two ready to go?

Rachel: I'm ready, but Joey's not even dressed yet!

Dad: Joey, come on! Today's the birthday of the world. It's a time to think about how we can be better people in the coming year. Running late isn't such a good way to begin the process.

Joey: Why do I have to wake up, get out of bed, and go hear someone blow a ram's ear? What can a shofar do to help me be better this year?

Rachel: It's a horn, not an ear!

Dad: Wait, Rachel, Joey's question is a good one. In fact, in Judaism, all serious questions are good questions!

Joey: So what's the answer? What can a shofar *do*?

Dad: Hmmm. Start getting dressed and I'll tell you a story that might explain it.

("Story" characters enter and stand on opposite side of stage from family.)

Dad: Once upon a time a peasant came upon a town just when a fire had broken out.

Townsperson 1: Help! Help! The inn down the road . . . it's on fire!

Townsperson 2: Did you say fire?

Townsperson 1: F-I-R-E!

Peasant: That spells fire.

Townsperson 1: Of course it spells fire! Call the drummer!

Drummer: Did someone say fire?

Townsperson 2: At last! Send the signal!

(Drummer beats loudly on drum, and soon all townspeople appear and form an assembly line carrying pails of water.)

Peasant: It's awfully strange that this man is playing a march when there's an inn on fire!

Child: Don't you see? His drumming is to put out the fire.

Peasant: Oh! Why didn't you say so?

Townsperson 1: Fire out!

Townsperson 2: Fire out?

Drummer: Fire out! *(He stops playing.)*

Peasant: Say, I'd like to take one of these drums back to my village. Where can I get one?

Dad: So the peasant bought a drum and returned to his village. A year later, a terrible fire broke out in his village.

Townsperson 3: Fire! Fire!

Peasant: Fire? No problem! I'll just beat on my drum.

Townsperson 4: Let's assemble! Form a line! Action!

Peasant: No, no, don't bother! I have this drum! As long as someone beats a drum, the fire will go out. Trust me, I've seen it work before.

Townsperson 3: Don't be silly. The drum is only to let us know of danger! Then we need to take action to stop the danger . . . in this case, the fire! Everybody! Quick! Get the water buckets!

Peasant: You mean the drum doesn't put out the fire?

Townsperson 4: Don't feel bad. The drum is very important. If we didn't hear its sound and wake up, we could never have put out the fire.

Dad: So of course the townspeople put out the fire and everyone lived happily ever after.

(Story people exit.)

Joey: Okay, Dad. But what does that have to do with getting up for services?

Dad: See, Joey, the shofar is like the drum. The shofar is sounded to wake us up . . .

Rachel: . . . and to let us know we better get working . . .

Dad: . . . working on being better people in the New Year.

Joey: So, you mean the shofar is like the drum because it can't solve the problem by itself.

Dad: Exactly!

Joey: But it makes us realize there is a problem to begin with.

Rachel: There's going to be a big problem if we're late to synagogue . . . how embarrassing!

Joey: Relax, Rachel. I'm almost ready. I don't take hours in the bathroom standing in front of the mirror before I go somewhere like some people I know.

Rachel: I don't take hours either and, besides, how would you know? You're always sleeping!

(Dad turns wastebasket over and plays it like a drum.)

Joey: Dad?

Rachel: Dad?

(Dad keeps playing.)

Joey: I think he's trying to wake us up to something.

Rachel: Yeah, I know. Sorry. I didn't mean to fight.

Joey: Me either. Sorry, Rachel. *(Pause.)* Okay, Dad, you can stop now.

Dad: I kind of like this . . . maybe in the New Year I can learn to play drums!

Rachel: Both of you, come on, I don't want to miss the shofar.

Joey: Me either.

Dad: Me either.

Kindness To
All Creatures

●●●

(Grades 1-3)

Cast of Characters

Narrator
Rabbi
Calf
Person 1
Person 2
Person 3
Person 4

Costumes

Calf can wear a simple sign saying "Calf" and doesn't need a
full animal costume. Other characters can be in simple dress.

(Narrator enters, rushing in.)

Narrator: Shalom, chaverim! Hello, friends! I do apologize for
being late. You see, I had to feed my animals before I came here
this morning. Now that might not seem so difficult to you, but I
have quite a collection of animals — five dogs, seven cats, 12
rats, 13 bats, 14 guinea pigs, 18 goldfish, 25 lizards . . . and,
yes, one rather finicky ferret. What can I say? Do any of you
have animals at home? Yes? *(Takes audience response.)* How
wonderful! How many of you help take care of your animals?
Feed them, walk them? Great! Did you know that being kind
to animals is a mitzvah? That's right, in Jewish law, we learn
to be kind to ALL living creatures — people and cats and bats
and rats and ferrets. ALL living creatures. So let me tell you a
little story.

(Rabbi enters on the opposite side of the stage, strolling along.)

Narrator: Once upon a time, there was a very wise Rabbi. He studied the Torah and all the sacred Jewish texts from sunrise to sunset. He wanted to be the best Jew, the kindest person he could be.

Rabbi: God has made such a beautiful world for us all. The Torah teaches us that the whole world is full of God's glory. I will show my love and thankfulness to God by being as kind as I can to all creatures.

Narrator: On this particular day, the Rabbi was on his way to town early, because it was Erev Yom Kippur. The whole town would come to synagogue to hear the chanting of the "Kol Nidre" prayer and to hear the Rabbi's words of wisdom. But just as the Rabbi was walking to the synagogue, he heard a noise.

Calf: *(From offstage.)* Moo-oo!

Rabbi: Moo to you! Where's that sound coming from?

Calf: *(Entering.)* Moo-ooo!

Rabbi: Little Calf, it's you! What are you doing on this road? There are no farms for miles around. This is the road into town.

Calf: I just wanted to take a little walk. I didn't mean to go so far out of the pasture. My mother was sleeping and didn't see me. Now I'm lost . . . and I'm very hungry . . . now I'll never see my mother again. Boo-hoo-moo!

Rabbi: There, there, little Calf. Don't worry, I'll help you get home. *(Pause.)* Say, I didn't know calves could cry. In fact, I didn't even know you could talk.

Calf: Of course we talk! And you understand us, Rabbi, because you are kind and care for all creatures.

Rabbi: Of course I do! We are all God's creatures.

23

Calf: So you will help me find my mother and get home?

Rabbi: Absolutely! I hope I can make it back to the synagogue in time for Kol Nidre. But the congregation will understand.

(They walk off together.)

Narrator: So the Rabbi took the Calf and they walked toward the countryside together. They had to walk quite a long way, because the little Calf had wandered far from his home. It was getting late. The sun was about to set. Still, the Rabbi could not find the Calf's home. Meanwhile, all the townspeople had gathered for Kol Nidre services.

(People enter.)

Person 1: I'm here nice and early, even before the Rabbi. I think I'll take a seat in the front row.

Person 2: It's not so early. It's time for services! Where is the Rabbi?

Person 3: It's not like him to be late!

Person 4: How could a Rabbi be late for Kol Nidre?

Person 1: That's right! We're all here on time. What's his excuse?

Person 2: Maybe something happened to him.

Person 3: Naaahh.

Person 4: Well, we can't very well start services without him. I wouldn't take the honor of leading this service.

Persons 1, 2, and 3: Me either.

Person One: Let's go find our Rabbi!

Persons 2, 3, and 4: Yes, let's!

(The people walk around stage, looking for the Rabbi.)

Narrator: So the people set off to find the Rabbi, for they very much wanted the Kol Nidre service to begin. They searched for him in town, but he was nowhere to be found. They searched for him in the countryside, but he was nowhere to be found. Finally, just as they were about to give up, they found him in a small barn far away from the synagogue.

(Rabbi and calf enter and People find them.)

Person 1: There he is! Our Rabbi!

Person 2: The Rabbi is in a barn? At this time? We're already late for Kol Nidre!

Person 3: What is the Rabbi doing so far away from town?

Person 4: Rabbi! What are you doing here?

Rabbi: Please, let me explain. I'm sorry to keep all of you waiting for services. But you see, I was walking to synagogue when I met this poor Calf who had wandered far from his mother. I'm sure you know that Jewish law teaches us to be kind to animals . . .

Person 1: That's true, but on Erev Yom Kippur?

Rabbi: What are we asking for on Yom Kippur? What do we pray for?

Person 2: We want to be inscribed in the Book of Life. We want to live for another year in this wonderful world God has created.

Rabbi: Yes, that's right. And Judaism teaches us to save all life, no matter what. How could I ask to be inscribed in the

Book of Life if I had not helped this little Calf get home? Without his mother's milk, he would surely have died.

Person 3: But this is a Calf. And we are people.

Person 4: But I see the Rabbi's point. We must try to save the lives of all creatures.

Rabbi: Yes, we must treat all life as sacred. So now, my friends, let us return to the synagogue and chant the "Kol Nidre."

(The people exit.)

Calf: Rabbi, I just want to thank you. It's so good to be home! I don't know what I would have done without you.

Rabbi: Don't mention it, little one. I think it will be a good year for all of us.

(Rabbi exits.)

Narrator: So you see, my friends, kindness to animals truly is a mitzvah. *(Pause.)* Oh dear, look at the time! I must go and walk my dogs, guinea pigs, and that finicky ferret! It has been so much fun seeing you all today. Shalom! L'hitraot!

Calf: *(Sticking his head out.)* Moo-oooo!

Narrator: Moo to you, too! Shalom!

The Ushpizin

(Grades 4-6)

Characters

Abraham
Isaac
Jacob
Joseph
Moses
Aaron
David
Sarah
Miriam

Costumes

Have fun with the costumes. Large name tags are a good way to identify the characters.

Staging

A bare set is fine for this play.

(All characters except Miriam and Sarah are on stage.)

Abraham: So, Sukkot begins tomorrow?

Isaac: Yes, Dad. Tomorrow is the 15th of Tishre.

Abraham: Time sure does fly!

Jacob: And on Sukkot, it really flies! Being one of the Ushpizin is lots of fun!

Joseph: Fun? It's better than anything I experienced in Egypt! The feasting is unreal!

Moses: You know, I may have to take it easy this year. Last year by Shemini Atzeret, I could barely fit into my robe.

Aaron: When you're one of the Ushpizin, brother Mo, you gotta eat. After all, we're special guests.

David: Who started that custom, anyway? I mean . . . of inviting a special guest for each of the seven days of Sukkot?

Abraham: I don't know . . . but whoever it was, I like 'em!

Isaac: I second that.

Jacob: And we're not just any old guest.

Joseph: That's right. We Ushpizin all have a special connection to Sukkot.

Moses: That's true. Sukkot is a time of remembering when we lived in the desert, when we had no permanent homes.

Aaron: I sure remember that experience!

David: Look at us — the patriarchs and leaders of Judaism — and we were all wanderers, all exiles!

Abraham: Yes. As you all know from the Book of Genesis, I left my father's home for an unknown land . . . when the Holy One promised to lead me.

Isaac: And then I, too, wandered all over the land of Canaan.

Jacob: There was a time when I ran away from you, Father. I went to uncle Laban, way up in Haran and worked for him — first for seven years, and then another seven, and then another six. And I would wander once again. Remember, I wandered as far as Egypt to live close to you, Joseph. My son, I never thought I'd see you again!

Joseph: I can't say I wandered to Egypt of my own free will, Dad. My brothers found a caravan to take me on my journey. But with God's help, I became a legendary exile!

Moses: But at least some good came out of the time in Egypt — we got to leave!

Aaron: And the wandering thing . . . believe me, I could write a book.

Moses: Someone already did, Aaron — a best-seller.

Aaron: Oh, well. I'm more suited for priestly duties anyhow.

David: Wow, we all *do* have a lot in common. I'm sure you remember how I had to flee from King Saul.

Abraham: So after all this fleeing, all this wandering, it's a good thing someone's finally having us for dinner.

Isaac: Being Ushpizin, special invited guests for dinner, isn't bad at all.

(Miriam and Sarah enter.)

Sarah: So, what is this? Golf day?

Jacob: Tomorrow's Sukkot. We'll be Ushpizin. We were just making dinner plans.

Miriam: You hear that, Sarah? Dinner plans? Yeah, I guess you and I didn't do our fair share of wandering.

Sarah: Do I have stories of shlepping! When God calls you to a new land, guess who gets stuck with the packing?

Miriam: You're telling me, sister!

Sarah: Well, we did get our fair share of dinner invitations last Sukkot.

Miriam: Absolutely! Lots of good casseroles, potlucks . . .

Sarah: Hot tea, chocolate!

Miriam: Oh, yeah! We should call all the gals — Rachel, Rebekah, Leah, Abigail, Hannah, Tamar, Esther — and make our own Ushpizin plans.

Sarah: You're right! I know a few sukkot we must visit again! There was a pumpkin pie just outside of Chicago that was to die for!

Miriam: I'm thinking of that potato dish we ate in Missouri!

Sarah: We'll make a list — come on, let's go!

Miriam: See you guys later! Chag Sameach!

Sarah: L'hitraot!

Men: *(Slightly startled.)* B-Bye!

Joseph: You get the sense they're making a whole science of this thing?

Moses: Unbelievable. One sukkah is sort of like the next one for me.

Aaron: Maybe they would let us tag along.

David: We could catch them if we run.

Abraham: For everyone's information, I did help with the packing when we set off on our journey.

Isaac: Dad, come on, give it a rest.

Abraham: All right, let's go!

Jacob: This will be one great year for us Ushpizin — come on!

(They exit.)

The Miracle of Eight

(Grades 1-4)

Characters

Shamash
Candle 1
Candle 2
Candle 3
Candle 4
Candle 5
Candle 6
Candle 7
Candle 8

Costumes

Candles might wear bright solid colors. They put on a gold crown (simple foil will work) when "lit" by the Shamash (who wears a crown when the play begins).

(The Shamash and Candles are on stage, lined up in a "chanukiah" position.)

Shamash: Well, crew, this is it. "Zote Chanukah," as they say.

Candle 1: "Zote Chanukah?" Who says that?

Shamash: Well, just about everybody . . . tonight anyway. "Zote Chanukah" means "this is Chanukah." The eighth night, the last night. This is it for the whole year.

Candle 2: Yeah, sure . . . this is the last night. But what does "Chanukah" mean?

Candle 3: Come on, we all know what Chanukah means! It means people have fun, eating latkes, spinning dreidles . . .

Candle 4: Getting presents!

Candle 5: Lots of presents! On Chanukah, I wouldn't mind being a person. I mean . . . not that it could ever compare to being a candle . . . but on Chanukah, it wouldn't be so bad.

Candle 2: But what does "Chanukah" really mean?

Candle 6: It means that we have an important job to do. We candles give light on very dark winter nights.

Candle7: It means we provide warmth — we make a room cozy.

Candle 8: Chanukah means that people are happy. They sing and celebrate, and our job is to make them even happier.

Candle 1: It means we light up the outside, too, when we shine through the window.

Shamash: Have the other candles answered your question, Candle 2?

Candle 2: Not exactly.

Shamash: They tried, but let's see if I can help. After all, "Zote Chanukah." They're all correct. We do play a very important role by providing light. But it's not just any old light. It's Chanukah light. And what does the word "Chanukah" mean?

Candle 1: Beats me.

Candle 3: Hmmm . . . I never thought about that.

Candle 4: I guess it would be good to know.

Shamash: Chanukah means "dedication."

All Candles: *(Together.)* Aaa-haa!

Candle 5: Well, that clears that up.

Candle 2: Dedication?

Shamash: You've all heard the story about the brave Maccabees, right?

Candle 5: They're the Jewish guys who fought the Syrian-Greeks who wanted to make the Jews pray to idols?

Candle 6: Right! The Maccabees fought hard and won the Temple back so the Jews could worship freely without anyone telling them what to do.

Shamash: Exactly! But you see, when they won the Temple back, it was in bad shape. No, lousy shape. No, awful shape. No, worse than awful. How can I put this nicely? *(Pause.)* It was all but destroyed!

All Candles: Destroyed?

Candle 7: Wait, wait . . . I know what happened. The Maccabees went into the destroyed Temple. They wanted to fix things up. They found a little bit of oil to light the Ner Tamid. Enough for maybe one day.

Candle 8: And so they lit the Eternal Light and they went to get more oil. But, of course, it took a while because the whole city was in bad shape from the battle. But that little bit of oil — enough for one day — lasted for eight whole days!

Candle 2: You mean until more oil could be found and brought to the Temple?

Shamash: That's right. That little bit of oil . . . well, it was a miracle.

All Candles: A miracle!

Shamash: That's why we call this holiday Chanukah — dedication. After a terrible thing happened, a holy place was destroyed, and with a little bit of oil the Temple was brought back to life. The Maccabees were dedicated to their task, and the Temple was rededicated to God.

Candle 2: So here we are. "Zote Chanukah."

All Candles: "Zote Chanukah!"

Shamash: We better get started, the sun is all but down.

Candle 2: Shamash?

Shamash: Yes, Candle 2?

Candle 2: I know I'm only a little candle. And this chanukiah — it's not in the Temple. It's just in someone's living room window. And they are having a great Chanukah — singing songs, playing dreidle . . .

Shamash: What's your point, Candle 2?

Candle 2: Well . . . I was wondering. Is this Chanukah, our Chanukah, a dedication?

Shamash: What do you think, Candle 2?

Candle 2: I don't know. That's why I'm asking.

Shamash: I think you do know. Tell me, is this Chanukah a dedication?

Candle 2: Well, with our light — our little light — we are reminding people that a great miracle occurred.

Shamash: Yes, Candle 2 — a great miracle occurred there.

Candle 2: I think . . . it *is* a dedication.

All Candles: "Zote Chanukah!"

(Shamash moves from left to right, "lighting" each candle by standing in front of each, while the candle places a crown on his/her head. When all are lit, they sing "Ma'oz Tzur.")

The New Year for Trees

(Grades 7-10)

Characters

Josh
Tree
Rabbi Ellen
Grandma 1
Grandpa 1
Grandma 2
Grandpa 2
Adam
Eve

Costumes and Staging

The Tree can be created by pasting some green leaves on a
brown T-shirt. Because the Tree is essentially an imaginary
character, it need not attempt to act in a realistic manner.

(The Tree is on stage. Josh enters.)

Josh: Hmmm . . . Tu B'Shevat . . . the New Year for trees. I
always thought that sounded a little goofy. I mean trees are
nice and all, but why can't they have the same New Year as the
rest of us?

Tree: Maybe the trees don't want the same New Year as the
rest of you!

Josh: Huh? What? Who said that? *(Looks around, but no one is
there.)* Ruth, was that you? Sandy? Adam? Amanda? Peter?
(Pauses, shrugs.) Oh, well, maybe I was just hearing things.

Tree: Maybe not.

Josh: Okay, who's hiding? Mrs. Cohen said we were each to
find our own tree, far away from each other. She said we

couldn't really study a tree if we were talking to each other. So bug off! This assignment is hard enough to do without any distractions. Study a tree. Look at it differently. *(Sees tree.)* Leaves . . . a trunk . . . roots . . . branches . . . yep, it's a tree. Nothing I haven't seen before.

Tree: You think you've seen it all. Boy, are you wrong.

Josh: I'm not wrong — I've seen plenty of trees. In fact, I . . . I . . . wait. Hey, who are you?

Tree: I said it once and I'll say it again. You think you've seen it all. And you're wrong.

Josh: This isn't funny! *(Starts to look in leaves, around trunk, etc.)* Who is it? Adam, if this is your idea of a joke . . .

Tree: Listen, young man! There's no one hiding from you. I'm right in front of you.

Josh: What? Where?

Tree: You were sent to study me, but you won't even listen to me. You've barely looked at me.

Josh: Wait. I must be hearing things.

Tree: You are. You're hearing the voice of your imagination. Imagination is a fascinating thing. In your imagination, Joshua, you are having a conversation with a tree!

Josh: But trees can't talk!

Tree: Of course trees can't talk! What are you, crazy? But in the world of your imagination, anything is possible. And you obviously need some inspiration to tackle this assignment.

Josh: Who wouldn't? I mean, trees are really kind of boring. They give us wood for building and fruit to eat. I don't mean to be disrespectful. It's just that this assignment is really hard.

Tree: Perhaps you need to think about trees as metaphors. Look at trees beyond what they give in concrete terms.

Josh: Metaphor? Isn't that something in poetry? I don't know anything about that . . . except for what I had to learn to pass my English test.

Tree: Metaphors are in poetry, Joshua, and they are also all around you. A metaphor is when you compare two unlike objects and find out what they have in common.

Josh: As in, my little sister is a monster.

Tree: Correct. Very good.

Josh: That was easy, but I don't know any tree metaphors.

Tree: Well, you think you don't, but in the deepest part of your imagination you know quite a few.

Josh: I do?

Tree: Yes, absolutely!

Josh: Really?

Tree: I guarantee it!

Josh: Then show me one!

Tree: Then show you one what?

Josh: Show me one metaphor!

Tree: Show me one metaphor what?

Josh: Show me one metaphor about a tree!

Tree: Show me one metaphor about a tree what?

Josh: About a tree what . . . what . . . what . . . what else do you want?

Tree: Will you show me one metaphor about a tree . . . pretty, pretty, pretty . . .

Josh: Oh, that. PLEASE!

Tree: Certainly. Though few people realize it, one's imagination responds very well to good manners.

Josh: Can we get on with it . . . umm . . . please?

Tree: Very well.

(Rabbi and Ellen enter holding a Torah.)

Josh: Hey! That's my cousin Ellen and the Rabbi. Ellen's holding the Torah like she did at her Bat Mitzvah!

Ellen and Rabbi: Eytz Chayim Hee . . .

Tree: Do you know what Eytz Chayim Hee means?

Ellen: It is a tree of life to them who hold fast to it and all its supporters are happy. Its ways are ways of pleasantness and all its paths are peace.

Josh: She's talking about the Torah, not about a tree.

Rabbi: Mazel Tov, Ellen! Your Torah reading was flawless! Now, as part of the Bat Mitzvah service, Ellen will share some thoughts with you about what she has learned.

Ellen: Thank you, Rabbi. When I first began studying for my Bat Mitzvah, I was sort of scared to read Torah. It always looked so hard to do. But having prepared my parashah, I'm really happy I did it. I see now why we compare the Torah to a tree of life when we return it to the Ark.

Tree: Metaphor! Metaphor! Metaphor!

Ellen: A tree provides all the things we need to survive. If there were no trees, our carbon dioxide wouldn't be absorbed and we wouldn't get oxygen. That's basic survival. And so, like a tree, the Torah gives us stories and instructions on how to live. Without that, how could we survive?

Josh: Wow! I never thought of that before! The Torah is the tree of life . . . that makes sense.

Rabbi: Yasher kochayeh, Ellen! May you go from strength to strength!

(Rabbi and Ellen exit.)

Josh: Wait! Where are they going? Her Bat Mitzvah isn't over! We didn't even get to the party.

Tree: They appeared in your imagination, Josh, just like my voice, and they can go as quickly as they came. So, a tree is like the Torah and the Torah is like a tree. Have you ever thought about that before?

Josh: No, not really. Hey, I have my metaphor now. I can go back to class. That wasn't so hard!

Tree: Not so fast! Once you activate your imagination, it's not so easy to stop.

Josh: You mean I have to learn more metaphors?

(Grandma 1, Grandpa 1, Grandma 2, and Grandpa 2 enter.)

Grandparents: Joshie, Baby! So good to see you! How are you? You look a little thin!

Josh: Grandma! Grandpa! Grandma! Grandpa! What are you doing here?

Grandpa One: Josh, my boy, that's simple! We're part of your family tree!

Josh: My what?

Grandma 1: Your family tree. That's another metaphor.

Grandpa 2: Look at these branches, Josh. See, my family, the family I was born into, represents one branch of your family.

Grandma 2: And my family is another branch. Then Grandpa and I met and we "went out on a limb" to be married. We formed our own little branch.

Grandparents: Awwww.

Grandma 1: It seems like just yesterday.

Grandpa 1: Josh, I can trace our family tree back to your great-great-great-great-great Grandpa!

Josh: But wait . . . how exactly are families like trees?

Grandparents: How are families like trees?

Grandpa 2: Okay, kid, let's take your immediate family. Mom, Dad, you, and little sister.

Josh: Little monster?

Tree: Ahem.

Grandma 2: You are each individuals — you are each a leaf. But you live on the same twig — you live in the same house.

Grandma 1: You eat from the same kitchen — or from the same water source as a family of leaves would.

Grandpa 1: And your twig connects to another twig of leaves — say, your cousins, your father's sister's family . . .

Grandpa 2: And those twigs are on the same branch and it goes on and on!

Grandma 2: As big as your family gets, darling, and as individual as each leaf may be, you still have the same roots.

Josh: What about the trunk? What does that represent?

Tree: Take a stab at it, Josh. Create your own metaphor!

Josh: Well . . . maybe what connects all the people to their roots . . . maybe the trunk is . . . maybe the trunk is God.

Grandparents: Whhhoah. Deep.

(Grandparents exit.)

Josh: Hey wait!

Tree: They're leaving, Josh. It's clear you can look at trees and see them in many different ways. So, if you're ready to go back to class, I'll be on my way.

Josh: Wait! Don't go! This is fun!

Tree: Fun? You said trees were boring. Fruit, shelter, what more is there to see?

Josh: Okay, come on, so I wasn't thinking too clearly. But I'm beginning to understand metaphors now. They're cool! I want more!

Tree: As the voice of your imagination, I'm actually a bit exhausted. Really, Josh, it's been splendid and maybe we can . . .

Josh: Don't go!

Tree: L'hitraot! Adios! See ya!

(Tree exits.)

Josh: Well, I guess I should go back to class. I wonder if anyone else has finished the assignment. Amanda? Amy? Adam?

Adam: *(Entering.)* Yes?

Josh: Who are you?

Adam: I'm Adam. I heard someone calling me.

Josh: Oh, yeah, that was me. I was looking for my friend Adam.

Adam: There's another Adam?

Josh: Yeah, there are lots of Adams in my school. There are three in my class.

Adam: Hmmm. So much to learn.

(Eve enters.)

Eve: Where were you? As if it's not bad enough that we were kicked out of Eden, you're not helping me with directions out here at all!

Adam: Don't get me started on Eden, Eve! It was your idea to eat from the Tree of Knowledge . . .

Eve: But the snake got me to do it. And did I force you?

Josh: Wait a minute . . . you guys aren't . . .

Adam: *(Extending hand.)* Adam.

Eve: *(Makes a curtsy.)* Eve. A pleasure.

Josh: No, the pleasure is mine! Umm, see, for my Religious School class we're studying Tu B'Shevat . . . you probably don't know what that it is . . . but never mind . . . and, see, we're supposed to look at trees . . . and, well, I thought I knew everything there was to know about trees . . . but of course I really didn't, and so my imagination kicked in and I'm thinking about tress metaphorically.

Adam and Eve: Say what?

Josh: Well, never mind. What I was wondering was . . . this Tree of Knowledge thing. Could we . . . you know . . . talk about it a bit?

Adam: Sure, join us, we haven't been talking about anything else since . . .

Eve: Let me tell you my side. What was your name again?

Josh: Josh.

(Josh pauses, as they walk toward the exit.)

Josh: *(Yelling.)* Mrs. Cohen, I'm really into this metaphor thing! This assignment was great!

Adam: Josh, come on! I really need to tell someone else my side!

Eve: Is that the only side that matters? I have a voice, too, you know.

Josh: Uh . . . so . . . Mrs. Cohen, I'll turn in the assignment next week. I promise!

Adam and Eve: Josh!

Josh: I gotta go!

(They exit together.)

The Four Children

(Grades 4-6)

Cast of Characters

Judy
Wicked Child
Wise Child
Simple Child
Child Who Doesn't Know How to Ask

List of Props

A small cot or chairs set up to look like a bed
A pillow

Costumes

Each child can wear a sign indicating his/her character.

(Judy lies in bed, center stage, tossing and turning.)

Judy: Mah, mah nish . . . mah nish what? Ohhh! Tomorrow's Pesach, and I can't even remember the first question! This isn't fair! Why do I have to sing the Four Questions at the Seder every year? Just because I'm the youngest of all my cousins? It's not fair. Mah nish, mah nish. Oh, maybe if I try to sleep, I'll remember in the morning.

(She lays her head on the pillow, closes her eyes, and snores loudly.)

Judy: *(In her sleep.)* Mah nishtanah halilah hazeh.

(The Wicked Child enters.)

Wicked Child: Judy, why are you asking those questions in your sleep? What does it mean to *you?*

Judy: *(Waking up.)* Huh, what, who are you?

Wicked Child: I'm the Wicked Child, from your Haggadah.

Judy: What are you doing in my room? How did you get in?

Wicked Child: Relax. You're only dreaming. Boy, you must really be worried about learning those Four Questions. You feeling kind of foolish?

Judy: Not foolish. It's just hard to say them when everybody's watching you.

Wicked Child: What does this whole Seder thing mean to you, anyway?

Judy: It's Pesach, you know.

Wicked Child: I don't see what the big deal is. The Jews were freed from slavery. But what does that have to do with me?

Judy: Well, you see . . .

Simple Child: *(Entering.)* Hi, Judy! Are you enjoying this dream?

Judy: I guess so.

Simple Child: I heard you were going to explain about the Seder, so I came in. I'm the Simple Child. I can never figure out what Pesach's all about.

Judy: I'll try my best to explain. You see, everywhere around the world, Jewish people gather to tell the story of the Exodus from Egypt.

Simple Child: What does "Exodus" mean?

Wicked Child: Ah, who cares? Why bother learning big words?

45

Judy: You should bother, it's very important! You see, when the Jews lived in Egypt, they were slaves. That means they had to do all the work their masters told them to do. They could only go certain places and weren't allowed to do lots of things they wanted. They had to work hard or they were punished.

Wicked Child: Yeah, yeah, yeah. That was a long time ago.

Judy: Please listen, maybe you'll learn something. The Exodus means that the Jews were able to leave Egypt because Moses . . .

Simple Child: I've heard of him — he was in a movie!

Judy: Yes, Moses was a good guy! He went to Pharaoh and said, "Let my people go!"

Simple Child: And that worked?

Wicked Child: I doubt it!

Judy: Not exactly. That's when God helped the Jewish people by causing the plagues to come down.

Simple Child: What are plagues?

Judy: You know, grasshoppers and frogs and annoying stuff like that. God caused them to fall on Egypt until Pharaoh agreed to let the Jews go.

Simple Child: Wow! Good story. But what does that have to do with why we get together and eat matzah ball soup?

Wise Child: *(Entering.)* Good question. There is so much to learn about Pesach! Every year, I ask about the details of the Seder rituals, and every year I have lots of new things to learn.

Judy: Hey! Who are you? Am I still dreaming?

Wise Child: To the best of my knowledge, you are dreaming, Judy. But that's okay. We learn a lot of things in our dreams.

Wicked Child: Oh, brother! What's with this guy?

Wise Child: I'm the Wise Child. I come to the Seder to learn all I can about Pesach. The Exodus was a long time ago, and Jews have been telling the story ever since. I want to learn about this part of my heritage and help the Jewish tradition continue. Besides, our teachers tell us that each one of us is supposed to imagine that we, ourselves, were slaves in Egypt and were led to freedom.

Wicked Child: Not me! I've never been to Egypt in my life! The farthest I've traveled is Disneyland!

Wise Child: We are to imagine what it was like being a slave, having no freedom. We should imagine seeing the ten plagues and following Moses to the Sea of Reeds. We can imagine God parting the Sea and the Hebrews crossing over and dancing with Miriam on the other shore.

Simple Child: Wow! But what does that have to do with matzah ball soup?

Wise Child: The special food we eat at the Seder helps to tell the story of the Exodus. You see, the Israelites had to leave Egypt in a hurry. They didn't have time to let bread rise, so they made it out of unleavened dough and baked it on the run, so to speak. We eat matzah — and matzah ball soup — to remember their escape.

Simple Child: Wow! I learned something new today. Thank you, Wise Child. And thank you, Judy, for having this dream.

Wicked Child: Even I have to admit, I do like that matzah ball soup. I guess Passover's not so bad. Thanks, Judy.

Judy: No problem. I'm feeling much more excited about asking the Four Questions tomorrow. Thank you, Wise Child. You sure know a lot. I'm really going to pay attention at the Seder so I can learn like you.

Wise Child: Best of luck, Judy. Just remember, we all have something new to learn every day of our lives. Now, we should go so you can get some sleep. Next time, you could try counting sheep instead of reciting the Four Questions. That always helps me.

Judy: Chag Samayach, all of you!

(They start to exit and Judy lies back down. The Child Who Doesn't Know How to Ask enters.)

Child Who Doesn't Know How to Ask: Uh, umm, sorry I'm late. I wasn't sure when to come in.

Judy: Who are you?

Child: I'm umm, uh.

Wise Child: That's the Child Who Doesn't Know How to Ask. This Child is also an important part of the Haggadah.

Judy: What's wrong? You look scared. Here, come sit on my bed.

Child: I really like Pesach, it's just so confusing. I don't know why we gather together or do what we do. And I'm too shy to ask. Everyone else knows exactly what's going on.

Simple Child: No, we don't. Even the Wise Child learns new things each year.

Child: But you have to ask to learn, and I just don't know how.

Judy: Wise Child, please help the Child Who Doesn't Know How to Ask. It's really a shame.

Wise Child: I think you can help, Judy.

Judy: Me? How?

Wise Child: We recite certain prayers because they explain the Seder, so even those people afraid to ask questions can learn about the Exodus. You know one of the most important parts of the Seder.

Judy: Me? You must be joking.

Wise Child: *(Whispering loudly.)* Mah Nishtanah.

Child Who Doesn't Know How to Ask: Please, Judy, will you share it with me?

Simple Child: Wow! The Child Who Doesn't Know How to Ask . . . just asked!

Judy: These are the Four Questions. They begin with this statement: How Different this night is! Now, here they are: Why do we eat matzah instead of bread? Why do we eat bitter herbs? Why do we dip herbs twice? And why do we sit in a reclining position during the reading of the Haggadah?

Simple Child: And if I listen to the Haggadah being read, I'll find out the answers?

Wise Child: That's right. And you might even feel as if you yourself have traveled from slavery to freedom.

Simple Child: From Egypt to the Promised Land.

Wicked Child: And you'll get a big bowl of matzah ball soup!

All togther: Yay!

Judy: Thank you. Each one of you has helped me to prepare for Pesach. I know it's important how well I sing the Four Questions, but it's just as important that they be asked. Boy, am I lucky I'm the youngest! My cousins don't know what they're missing.

All Four Children: *(Leaving.)* Chag Samayach, Judy!

Judy: *(Lying down on bed.)* Bye-bye! *(As she falls asleep.)* Mah nishtanah halilah hazeh me kol halaylote . . .

Miriam the Prophet

(Grades 4-6)

Characters

Miriam
Yocheved
Pharaoh's Daughter
Professor Meshugenah
Amnon

Staging

This play becomes a "play within a play" as the Professor tells his story. Characters can add costume pieces or act in a more theatrical style to denote this. Although the biblical characters are obviously "old," they play as contemporary people.

(Miriam is on stage.)

Miriam: *(Singing to herself.)* Il lu hotzi hotzi anu, hotzi anu mimitzraim, hotzi anu mimitraim, Dayenu! Da-da-yaynu, da-da-yaynu-da-da . . . eh . . . oh! Excuse me! I didn't see you all sitting there. I just love to sing, especially that song! Do you know what Dayaynu means? Anyone? *(Takes responses from audience.)* That's right — it would have been enough. When God brought us, the Israelites, out of Egypt, out of slavery — well, that would have been enough. But God did so much more for us. For instance, God made the waters of the Sea part! Can you imagine seeing such a miracle? Believe me, it was . . . it was simply . . . well, MIRACULOUS! That's why I couldn't help myself. I started singing and dancing and soon all the women began following me and we danced all night after crossing the sea! *(Pause.)* Oh, I'm sorry. I forgot to introduce myself. My name is Miriam the Prophet. Have you ever heard of me? *(Takes responses from audience.)*

Yocheved: *(Entering.)* Excuse me, darling, but I think you should explain to the boys and girls how you became a prophet.

Miriam: Oh, Mother, come on. I'm sure all of them know about that. It's nothing special. After all, the Jewish people have had many other prophets. Like Elijah, for instance. Have you all heard of Elijah? *(Takes audience responses.)*

Yocheved: I know you're not the only prophet, but you are a very, very special prophet. And I'm not saying that just because you're my little girl.

Miriam: Mother, I'm not a little girl! I've been a prophet of the Jewish people for over three thousand years!

Yocheved: Well, you'll always be a little girl to me. I remember when your baby brother Moses was born . . . how you helped me bathe and diaper him. And then when I placed him in the cradle of bulrushes, you watched him float in the river.

Pharaoh's Daughter: *(Entering.)* Until I found him and picked him up out of the basket and held him close to my heart! What a sweet baby he was.

Miriam: Bat Pharaoh! Pharaoh's daughter! You look wonderful.

Yocheved: It's been such a long time . . .

Pharaoh's Daughter: *(Kissing them.)* You both look great. Really, Yocheved, you haven't changed a bit. I remember how you used to come to our palace and nurse baby Moses.

Yocheved: All because this one, my Miriam, followed you and told you she knew of a nurse.

Miriam: Mom, please, you're embarrassing me.

Yocheved: But all of it is true — you acted like a prophet from the time you were a little girl. You were always brave and strong and compassionate.

Miriam: Mom, stop.

Pharaoh's Daughter No, Miriam, let her kvell. It's all true, what a brave little girl you were. Even though my father, the Pharaoh, had ordered all Israelite baby boys to be killed, when I picked up baby Moses and especially when I saw you, his older sister, watching over him so protectively, I just couldn't let any harm come to him.

Miriam: How did you know I was his sister?

Yocheved: It's obvious, you both have my eyes.

Pharaoh's Daughter Look, I know it's been a long time since you left Egypt, but when I heard that there would be a telling of your story, of how you became a prophet, I just couldn't miss it!

Miriam: Would everyone stop with all the prophet business? All I know is, I've lived my life the best I could. And that means I've always spoken — and sung — the truth from my heart.

Yocheved: And that's exactly what makes you a prophet, sweetie.

Miriam: Whatever.

Pharaoh's Daughter So. When will the story begin?

Professor Meshugenah: *(Entering.)* Shalom, shalom, shalom! How's everybody doing tonight? You know, I just flew in from Tel Aviv and, boy, are my arms tired!

Yocheved: Professor Meshugenah, at last. We've been waiting for you.

Miriam: Who is this man?

Yocheved: Why, it's Professor Meshugenah, the world's leading expert on midrash.

Professor Meshugenah: Psssttt . . . Yocheved . . . I hate to disappoint you, but I'm actually the world's second best expert on midrash. The real expert is Amatta.

Yocheved: Well, I ordered the number one expert to come today! So, what's Amatta?

Professor Meshugenah: Nothing! What's amatta with you? Heh heh heh. Actually, she's my twin sister, Professor Amatta.

Yocheved: Next time, I won't order a professor from the Home Shopping Network.

Miriam: Mom, how could you?

Yocheved: It seemed like a bargain.

Professor Meshugenah: Ladies, ladies, ladies, settle down and let's begin. Yes, I did once have aspirations of becoming a stand-up comic, but all the perspiration that comes with the job turned me off. Besides, midrash is much, much more interesting than playing in Vegas.

Pharaoh's Daughter Excuse me, but what exactly is midrash?

Professor Meshugenah: Hey, hey, ho, ho! I swear, ladies and gentleman, she was not a plant! What is midrash? Funny you should ask, cause even funnier, I'm gonna tell you. Midrash, my friends, comes from the Hebrew word root "drash," meaning to search, to explain, to seek out. So when the Rabbis of old would drash on a text of Torah, they would seek out the hidden meaning of each phrase, each word.

Miriam: And sometimes, they would take a phrase or a sentence and elaborate, add more, make up their own story based on the text. And that is what we call midrash.

Professor Meshugenah: Hey, who's getting paid here — you or me?

Yocheved: Professor, you'll have to remember, my daughter is a prophet.

Professor Meshugenah: Yeah, yeah, yeah. Well, I may not have sung at the Reed Sea, but I do sing in my shower! (*Sings in operatic style.*) O, solo mio . . .

Miriam: Professor, we all have the qualities of the prophets. That's why we're gathered here today. I want to share this midrash with all of these people, so that they can see that they, too, can be prophets.

Professor Meshugenah: Really? Everyone? Even . . . even . . . someone who was kicked out of his sixth grade talent show for not being funny?

Miriam: Let's tell the story and you decide for yourself.

Yocheved: I'll begin. Oh wait. Where is Amnon, my husband? We need him here to tell the story.

Miriam: You're right, Mom. Dad! Dad! Where are you?

Yocheved: That's just like him, late to every occasion.

Amnon: (*Entering.*) Sorry I'm late. Hi, everyone. Yocheved, my lovely wife. Miriam, my beautiful daughter. And say, aren't you the Princess?

Pharaoh's Daughter That's right.

Amnon: Long time no see. Well, I guess we can begin. Who's this guy?

Professor Meshugenah: You've heard of Albert Einstein?

Amnon: Sure, the physicist.

Professor Meshugenah: Well, I'm not him.

Yocheved: That's Professor Meshugenah. He's a top expert on midrash. At least that's what the Home Shopping Network said.

Amnon: Yocheved, I told you to stop ordering off the Internet.

Yocheved: So this was the last time . . .

Professor Meshugenah: Excuse me! I would love to stay and hear you discuss my merit, but my contract says I'm here to share the story of how Miriam became a prophet. And that's it. I have other places to be you know. Important places. Later this evening, I'll be leading a post-show discussion of *Joseph and the Amazing Technicolor Dreamcoat*.

Miriam: Professor, good for you, speaking up for yourself like that! I knew you could do it!

Professor Meshugenah: Thank you, Miriam. Actors to places. And so, we begin with the story of how Miriam became a prophet. All of you, off stage! Spotlight, bevakashah! *(Pause.)* In the time of Pharaoh, the Israelite people were enslaved. Hardship after hardship came upon them. They toiled with bricks and mortar, making store cities for Pharaoh. But Pharaoh was still troubled. He saw the Israelite people increasing — even in slavery they were still thriving. So he ordered the slaughter of any Israelite baby boy born from that day on!

(Yocheved and Amnon enter, as if actors on a stage, oblivious to the professor.)

Yocheved: Amnon, what are we to do? Pharaoh keeps making things worse and worse for our people.

Amnon: I wish I could do something to change things, but I can't. Just yesterday, one of the Israelite slaves tried to rebel against an Egyptian taskmaster and was killed.

Yocheved: Right there on the construction site?

Amnon: Right before my eyes.

Yocheved: I'm worried for us, Amnon, but I'm more worried for our children, Miriam and Aaron. I don't want anything bad to happen to them.

Amnon: We can only trust God to protect them, Yocheved. We have no other way to help them. But we can save any children yet to be born.

Yocheved: Amnon, what do you mean?

Amnon: I mean that Pharaoh ordered all Israelite boys to be killed at birth. So we can't take the risk of bringing any more children into the world. The only way to make sure of that is for me to leave you.

Yocheved: Amnon, no, no, don't go!

Professor Meshugenah: Yocheved broke into tears as Amnon packed his things. But as he was about to leave, his young daughter Miriam jumped out of bed.

Amnon: Miriam, what are you doing up? Go back to your straw mat.

Miriam: Where are you going, Daddy?

Amnon: Just . . . out. Go back to sleep, honey.

Yocheved: Please, Amnon, at least tell her the truth.

Miriam: You don't have to. I already heard you talking. I thought I was having a bad dream, but I pinched myself and now I realize I'm awake.

Amnon: Miriam, honey, I don't want to leave you and Mommy and Aaron . . .

Miriam: You don't love us?

Amnon: Of course I do!

Miriam: Then you shouldn't leave.

Amnon: I'm leaving because I love you all. Don't you see? If your mother has another baby boy, they'll kill him and I cannot bear to see that happen.

Miriam: But what if Mom has a baby girl?

Amnon: What do you mean?

Miriam: If she has a baby girl, what will happen?

Amnon: Well, she would live and grow up just like you.

Miriam: Then you, Dad, are acting worse than Pharaoh. He ordered the death of all boys, but by leaving, you're killing the chance that we might have another girl. I thought you always taught Aaron and me that the Israelites believe in choosing life above all else?

Amnon: My wise little daughter. Yocheved, did you hear her?

Yocheved: Yes, yes. Miriam, you just spoke for me when my heart was trembling and broken.

Amnon: Miriam, you thought for me when my mind was clouded with fear.

Yocheved: Miriam, your truth is the truth of all the Israelite people.

Amnon: Miriam, you will grow to be very wise . . . to be a prophet.

Professor Meshugenah: And so Amnon unpacked his bags and though they were slaves, they were all a family again.

Yocheved: And I gave birth to a baby boy.

Miriam: And I helped you to make a cradle of bulrushes and I walked along as he floated in the river.

Pharaoh's Daughter: And I found him when I was bathing and raised him as a son.

Amnon: And my son grew to lead the Israelites out of Egypt.

Miriam: And my other brother Aaron became the High Priest of Israel.

Professor Meshugenah: And I . . . I'm gonna go for my dreams, after all! Thank you, Miriam. The truth in my heart is . . . I love midrash, but I also want to be a comedian. Do you think I can make it?

Miriam: What's black and parchment and read all over?

Professor Meshugenah: The Torah Scroll!

Miriam: Pretty quick, Professor. You'll make it, all right. Remember, we all have the ability to act like prophets . . . to listen to our hearts and speak the truth.

(All sing and dance to "Dayaynu.")

Kos Eliyahu

• •

(Grades 6-9)

Cast of Characters

Mom
Jonathan
Zayde
Great Grandma Rose
Stranger

Setting and Props

Table
Chairs
Kiddush cup
Plates, silverware, glasses, etc.
Tzedakah box
Envelope
Money (fake is okay)

Production Notes

When Zayde tells his story, the older characters appear but do not interact with the characters from the present time.

(Table and chairs are set on stage. Mom enters.)

Mom: Jonathan! Jonathan! Where are you?

Jonathan: *(Entering.)* I'm right here. What's wrong?

Mom: I asked you to set the table an hour ago. Please, everyone's going to be here for the Seder soon.

Jonathan: Well, Grandpa was telling me stories, and I lost track of time.

Mom: So let him tell you the stories while you set the table. I have 16 guests coming tonight. I need all the help I can get.

Jonathan: So I need to set up 16 places?

Zayde: *(Entering.)* Seventeen. Don't forget our most important guest.

Mom and Jonathan: Who?

Zayde: Eliyahu HaNavi!

Mom: That's right!

Jonathan: Eliyahu Hana-who?

Mom: He means Elijah. Set the special Kiddush cup — the Kos Eliyahu — at the head of the table. I need to check on the food. Your Dad is out picking up more matzah. Jonathan, you set the table . . . and Grandpa, you can . . .

Zayde: I'll help Jonathan. Don't worry — everything will be fine.

(Mom exits.)

Jonathan: Why do we always make such a big deal about pouring a special glass of wine for Eliyahu and opening the door for him? I mean, no one ever really comes in or drinks the wine. *(Pause.)* Once Dad tried to trick us by sipping it during the Seder, but I caught him.

Zayde: Jonathan, just because you've never seen Elijah the Prophet doesn't mean that someday he won't come and sit down at your Seder table. Eliyahu appears when you least expect it . . . sometimes when you need his help the most.

Jonathan: Zayde, come on. You don't really believe that, do you?

Zayde: Who am I to believe or not to believe? All I can tell you is, all over the world, Jewish people have at times encountered a mysterious stranger, who offers help without ever asking for something in return.

Jonathan: Yeah, well, maybe if I encountered the stranger, then I might believe this Eliyahu business.

Zayde: Yes. There is no question. When you meet Elijah, it changes you.

Jonathan: Why, Zayde? Have you met him?

Zayde: Maybe I have, maybe I haven't. The world works in mysterious ways.

Jonathan: Come on, Zayde . . . I know that means you have a story. Tell me!

Zayde: A story I have . . . what you make of it, is up to you.

Jonathan: So?

Zayde: So, when I was about your age, Jonathan, yes, I was 11 years old at the time, America was fighting a very important war. You've heard me tell you about World War II. So my father was away in Europe fighting and my mother, your Great Grandma Rose, had to take a job working in a factory. It was hard work and she came home very tired, but at least we always had food to eat.

(Benny appears on opposite side of stage. Great Grandma Rose enters)

Benny: Mama, you're home!

Great Grandma Rose: Hello, my darling. Did you have a nice day at school today?

Benny: It was pretty good.

Great Grandma Rose: Did you learn a lot of things?

Benny: We learned about the war. Hitler is doing bad things to the Jews, Mama.

Great Grandma Rose: I know, darling. That is why your father is away, fighting hard. And we must do all we can here to help them overseas. I wish I had money to send. There are places that are helping Jews to escape.

Benny: But, Mama, we hardly have enough money to buy food for ourselves!

Great Grandma Rose: Shah! We always have plenty. Let me look in the tzedekah box and see how much I have saved. Whenever I have extra coins, I drop them in.

(They freeze.)

Zayde: In that moment, I was paralyzed with fear. The truth was, there was no money in the tzedekah box. I had taken it. Not to spend frivolously, mind you. But my mother had put me in charge of all the shopping, and the money she gave me was never enough. I couldn't buy challah or candles or wine, all things we needed to celebrate Shabbat, with the money she gave me, so I took a little each week from the tzedekah box. It had been a few weeks since Mama had dropped in any coins.

Jonathan: So what did you do?

Zayde: Let me tell you.

(Focus back on the other characters.)

Great Grandma Rose: *(Opening empty tzedakah box.)* What is this? Where are my coins?

Benny: Mama, it was me . . . I've been taking them.

Great Grandma Rose: How could you? What were you buying . . . candy?

Benny: No . . . no, Mama . . . nothing like that! The money you give me — it's not enough to buy the groceries we need. I never have enough to buy candles or wine or . . .

Great Grandma Rose: Benny, you should have told me . . . we could have done without. I was saving that money for tzedakah . . . and also I invited the whole family over for a nice Seder. No one else has the money to do it. Now what will I tell them?

Benny: I'm sorry, Mama. I was just trying to do the right thing.

Great Grandma Rose: I know. I wish I didn't have to give you the responsibility of shopping and taking care of the house. But I can't do it when I must work at the factory so late. It will be different, God willing, when the war is over.

(A knock is heard.)

Great Grandma Rose: Who could that be? *(She answers the door and the stranger enters.)*

Stranger: Good evening, Ma'am. I'm sorry to bother you.

Great Grandma Rose: Yes, what do you want?

Stranger: I am going around the neighborhood collecting tzedakah for the Jews in Europe. There are efforts going on to help them escape.

Great Grandma Rose: Yes I know . . . I wish I could . . .

Stranger: A little something?

Benny: *(Angrily.)* Listen, mister, my mother doesn't have any money! She works all day long in a factory because my father is off in the army fighting the Nazis! She was saving up money for tzedakah . . . but I opened the tzedakah box and used her money. Now we have nothing to give.

Stranger: I see . . .

Great Grandma Rose: He's a good boy, really. We didn't have enough money to make Shabbos, so he took . . . I like him to have a nice Shabbos, you understand. In fact, I had invited my whole family to come for Seder in two nights, and I would invite you, too, but the money I was saving is gone. I have nothing.

Stranger: Well, I'm sorry to bother you and I didn't mean to upset you. Thank you for the invitation to your Seder . . . but I will be dining elsewhere.

(He exits. They freeze.)

Jonathan: Wow. So what happened? You didn't have a Seder that year?

Zayde: Not exactly. You see, the very next day when I got home from school, there was a knock at the door.

(They freeze and focus returns to Benny. A knock is heard.)

Benny: Who is it? What do you want?

Stranger: It's the gentleman who visited last night.

Benny: Yeah, well, my mother isn't home. And we don't have any money. We already told you that.

Stranger: Please open the door. I have a gift for your mother.

Benny: Fine. Hold on.

(He opens the door and the Stranger hands him an envelope.)

Stranger: Please give this to your mother. And Happy Pesach!

(He exits.)

Benny: Hmmm. I should wait for Mama. But there's something strange about this envelope. I better open it.

(He opens the envelope and takes out a thick wad of bills and a letter.)

Benny: *(Reading letter.)* Please accept this gift so you can make a lovely Seder for your family. By fighting in Europe, your husband is doing all he can to help the Jews there. And you are doing all that you can to work and support your family here. You are truly a blessed woman and the Holy One will watch out for you.

(Great Grandma Rose enters.)

Benny: Mama, what are you doing home?

Great Grandma Rose: I'm as surprised as you are. The boss let us leave early today, for no good reason. Just because we've been working so hard, he said.

Benny: Mama, that stranger . . .

Great Grandma Rose: That stranger? You know, I asked all the ladies at work today about him. It seems he didn't knock at one other door besides ours. I thought he said he was going all over the neighborhood. I think it's very suspicious.

Benny: Mama, he just came here. And he handed me this — for you.

Great Grandma Rose: What? Let me see.

(She takes the envelope, touches the bills, and reads the letter.)

Great Grandma Rose: Oh my! We can have a huge Seder now. Let's go to the store! I'll invite the neighbors.

Benny: But, Mama, who was that stranger? He didn't write his name on the letter or tell us.

Great Grandma Rose: The world works in mysterious ways, my son.

Benny: What do you mean?

Great Grandma Rose: I know many stories from the old country that my parents would tell. Sometimes when people needed help, they'd run into a mysterious stranger. And many believe that stranger is Eliyahu HaNavi.

Benny: Elijah the Prophet? You mean the guy we pour a glass of wine for?

Great Grandma Rose: The very one. Come darling, let's go to the store.

(They exit.)

Jonathan: Was it really Elijah, Zayde?

Zayde: Who knows? Anyway, we better set the table or it will take Elijah to save us from your Mother.

Mom: *(Entering.)* And is everything ready? Is the table set yet?

Zayde: It's my fault — we were talking. We'll start right now.

Mom: Take your time — when the guests come, you two will have some explaining to do.

(She exits and a knock is heard at the door.)

Jonathan: Who could that be? The Seder's not supposed to start for another hour.

Zayde: Let's see.

(He opens the door and the Stranger enters.)

Stranger: Hello. Sorry I'm so early.

Zayde: Don't be silly. Come in. You must be a friend of my daughter's. I'm Benjamin Cohen. I don't believe we've met.

Stranger: Oh yes. We've met.

Zayde: Oh, excuse me. At my age, the memory is the first to go.

Stranger: Well, it's been a while.

Jonathan: And I'm Jonathan.

Stranger: Good to meet you. So, let me help. May I set the table?

Jonathan: Do you like setting tables or something?

Stranger: I don't mind. I like to help out wherever I can. *(He proceeds to set table quickly and efficiently.)*

Jonathan: *(In a stage whisper.)* Psstt, Zayde, come here.

Zayde: Yes?

Jonathan: I've never seen that guy before. I don't think he's a friend of Mom and Dad's.

Zayde: I see.

Stranger: Well, there you go, the table's set. You know I really am rather early. I hate to be a rude guest and show up empty-handed. I think I'll go and get some flowers. See you in a bit — and may you both have a very happy Pesach.

(Stranger exits and Mom enters.)

Mom: Wow! The table looks gorgeous. I should have known you'd come through in the end. All right, I think I can relax now and get ready to enjoy the Seder.

Zayde: Look, even the wine is poured . . . I mean, we poured the wine.

Mom: You forgot to fill Kos Eliyahu. There's only a drop in here.

Jonathan: What?

Mom: Come look. Only a drop. That's strange — I'm sure I washed this glass, but it looks like someone drank from it. Well, fill it up. Eliyahu HaNavi deserves a whole glass.

Jonathan and Zayde: He sure does!

The Story of Ruth

(Grades 7-10)

Cast of Characters

Ruthie
Nancy
Rabbi
Elimelech
Naomi
Mahlon
Kilyon
Orpah
Ruth
Boaz

Costumes

The biblical characters may wear simple clothes (i.e., one color, plain dresses, etc.) to distinguish them from the contemporary characters.

Props

Chairs or desks for Ruthie and Nancy
Tanach
Doll

Setting

Stage should be set so that contemporary characters are downstage right or downstage left so that the biblical characters can play center stage.

Production Notes

This play is especially appropriate for Confirmation classes, but can be used to teach the Book of Ruth to any age group.

Scene 1

(Ruthie and Nancy sit at their desks. Rabbi enters.)

Rabbi: Nancy, Ruthie . . . I'm glad to see you're here early. I have a special task for you. As you know, your Confirmation will take place on Shavuot when we celebrate . . .

Ruthie: . . . the Israelites receiving the Torah on Mount Sinai.

Rabbi: That's right. Excellent. For one moment, all of Israel felt God's presence. And we can still feel God's presence when we read and study Torah. That's why I want to give you two this special project. You see, at Shavuot we celebrate God's giving us the Torah, but we also celebrate an agricultural festival, the wheat harvest. The Israelites would celebrate their bounty and bring a sacrifice of two loaves of bread made from the newly harvested wheat to the Temple.

Nancy: What does wheat have to do with the Torah?

Rabbi: What do you think?

Nancy: Well, I guess both the Torah and wheat nourish us — in different ways, I mean.

Rabbi: Excellent answer, Nancy! So, there is a special tradition on Shavuot that we read the Book of Ruth. The story takes place during the wheat harvest . . . and, well, I'd like to see you come up with some other reasons why we read the Book of Ruth on Shavuot. So, here's a copy. Take a look, and I'll be back in a while to talk about it with you.

(Rabbi exits.)

Nancy: I can't believe how much there is to do to get ready for Confirmation — practice leading services, learn to read Torah, write a speech, and now the Rabbi wants us to study the Book of Ruth . . .

Ruthie: Come on, Nancy, don't give up now. Let's just do what

70

the Rabbi says. We can read it to ourselves first, then try to put it in our own words. You start.

(As they open the book, the biblical characters enter and take their places.)

Nancy: All right, there was a famine in Bethlehem, in Judah, and so this guy Elimelech and his wife Naomi decide to take off.

Scene 2

Elimelech: Naomi, I hate to say this, but we're going to have to leave Judah.

Naomi: If we can't earn a living here, if we can't feed our family, we have no choice. I just hate the thought of leaving all the people we love and going to some strange place. But, my dear husband, there is no other choice.

Elimelech: I wish there was another way. *(Pauses.)* Let's tell Mahlon and Kilyon.

Naomi: Boys! Come here, we have news to share.

Mahlon: Don't worry. We're already packed.

Kilyon: We knew we'd have to leave. There's no wheat to harvest in Judah — the land is so dry.

Mahlon: I hear the land of Moab is pretty fertile and they need people to work in the fields.

Naomi: Let me pack a few more things and we'll go.

(When Ruthie and Nancy speak, the biblical actors freeze.)

Scene 3

Ruthie: I sure would hate to pick up and leave my home like that! Okay, so they went to the land of Moab and did all right earning a living, but Elimelech died. Oh, that's so sad. But

Mahlon and Kilyon each got married to Moabite women. One was named Orpah and one was Ruth. Like me! But then Mahlon and Kilyon died. Oh, that's *really* sad. Now Naomi was in Moab . . . without her husband or her sons.

Scene 4

Naomi: There is nothing left for me here in Moab. I've heard things are better now in Judah. I might as well go back there.

Orpah: We'll go with you. I love to travel — see new sights, meet new people! How about it, Ruth? We've never been to Bethlehem.

Ruth: Absolutely. I wouldn't think of letting you go alone, Naomi. Not after all you've done for me, especially since my husband died. You're like a mother to me!

Naomi: Don't be foolish. You two are both still young, and it's not going to be an easy trip back to Bethlehem. And Judah is quite different from Moab. We believe in one God there. You would be better to go back to your parents' homes, where you know the customs and know the people.

Ruth: Even though I was born in Moab, I, too, believe in one God.

Orpah: Hmm. I don't know.

Naomi: Let me also tell you . . . I don't know if any Israelite men will be interested in marrying widows. Stay in Moab, you'll each meet a nice Moabite man.

Orpah: You know, that's not a bad idea. I am still young. *(Pauses.)* It's been great knowing you, Naomi. But I should stay here. See you. Keep in touch. *(She hugs her and exits.)*

Naomi: You, too, Ruth. Go with your sister-in-law. Why hang around with an old lady?

Ruth: I'm not like Orpah, Naomi. Listen to me. Wherever you go, I will go. Wherever you stay, I will stay. Your people are my people. Your one God is my God. Wherever you will die, that's where I'll be buried, too. Only death will separate you and me.

Naomi: All right, then, if you're so sure. Let's take our few things and go. It's quite a trip back to Bethlehem.

Scene 5

(Nancy speaks and the characters freeze.)

Nancy: So Naomi and Ruth set off and they eventually made it back to Bethlehem at the time of the wheat harvest. People greeted them, but no one offered them any food or help. So Ruth decided she would go to the wheat fields and work.

Ruth: Maybe if I just stay at the very edge of the field, no one will notice me. I don't know if they'd appreciate a Moabite woman picking in their fields. But Naomi and I need to eat . . . and hard work doesn't bother me.

Boaz: *(Entering.)* Shalom, workers! May Adonai be with you!

Ruth: May Adonai be with you!

Boaz: Hello, there. I don't think I've seen you around here before.

Ruth: No, I'm not from here. I am Naomi's daughter-in-law and I traveled with her from Moab. I'm sorry just to show up in your field, but we have no food.

Boaz: Please . . . make yourself comfortable here. You can take as much wheat as you can pick . . . and come back tomorrow. And the next day! All through the harvest, you are welcome in my fields. Umm, what did you say your name was?

Ruth: I'm Ruth.

Boaz: And I'm Boaz. *(Pauses.)* Oh, and take a lunch break. We have cheese and fruit and lots of goodies just down the field over there.

Ruth: Boaz, may I ask . . . umm . . . why are you being so kind to me?

Boaz: From what I've heard, it's you who are kind. The word has gotten around about how you stayed with Naomi, how you left your homeland and came to this strange country out of love for her.

Ruth: And because I believe in one God, as you do here.

Boaz: We welcome you here, Ruth.

(They freeze.)

Scene 6

Nancy: Hey, this is getting good! So in the next part, Ruth goes home and tells Naomi about Boaz. And it turns out that Boaz is some relative of Elimelech's, and in those days, next of kin were supposed to marry a relative's widow.

Ruthie: So Ruth and Boaz get married?

Nancy: Yeah, and she and Naomi have plenty to eat and they're happy again. But wait, it gets even better . . .

Scene 7

(Ruth holds a small doll or towel wrapped to look like a baby.)

Ruth: Naomi, come here and look at your new grandson!

Naomi: I can't believe it! After all of our hardships, I never thought I'd live to see such a happy day!

Ruth: We will name him Oved.

Naomi: This baby will grow to do many wonderful things! I just know it.

Ruth: *(Kisses the baby.)* So do I.

74

(They exit.)

Scene 8

Nancy: It says here that Oved grew up and had a son named Jesse, and Jesse was the father of King David.

Ruthie: So if Ruth hadn't been brave enough to leave her home in Moab and go with Naomi, there wouldn't have been a King David.

Nancy: Right. *(Pause.)* So, why do you think we read this Book at Shavuot?

Ruthie: Well, the wheat harvest. That's clear.

Nancy: I think it's something else, too. The Book of Ruth is about the life of someone who really lives by Torah, even though she wasn't born a Jew. Ruth treats Naomi with kindness and love and helps her through hard times.

Ruthie: That's true. You're right, Nancy.

Nancy: I know I've been kind of grumpy about how much work Confirmation is. Thanks for keeping me going. I don't think I could have made it through this experience without you.

Ruthie: Hey, Nancy, we did it togther.

(Rabbi enters.)

Rabbi: Ruthie, Nancy, how is your studying going? Let's see if we can work through the Book of Ruth together.

Nancy: No problem, Rabbi. Ruthie and I can tell you all about it.

(They open the book as lights go down.)

The Rebbe and the Watchman

(Grades 7-10)

Cast of Characters

Narrator
Rebbe
Wife
Watchman
Son
Daughter
Student 1
Student 2
Woman

List of Props

Books for students
Flashlight for watchman
Chairs and table for family

Production Notes

This play, which is based on a Hasidic story, can be used as a good starting point for a discussion about God's presence in our lives.

(Narrator is on stage.)

Narrator: Once upon a time, in a land not so very far away, there lived a wise Rebbe. Can anyone tell me who exactly a Rebbe is, or what exactly a Rebbe does? *(Takes audience response.)* Very good! A Rebbe is many things, as you will see. A teacher. A problem solver. A helper. A friend. And so on.

Rebbe: *(Entering.)* Oy, with a list like that, no wonder I'm tired! I didn't realize I had so many jobs!

Narrator: Oh, yes, and probably more than that. Shall we show our friends in the audience here what a typical day in your life is like?

Rebbe: Why not? If you think it would be of interest, let's show!

Narrator: Very well, then. Without further, ado, we shall present "The Rebbe and the Watchman!" *(Pause.)* Rebbe, *(Clears throat.)* backstage, for places.

Rebbe: Backstage? Just point me which way. This show biz, it's so confusing! *(Exits with help of Narrator.)*

Narrator: As I was saying, once upon a time, in a place not so very far away, there lived a wise Rebbe. He would wake up every day, and say his morning prayers.

(Rebbe enters.)

Rebbe: *Modeh ani l'fanecha . . .*

Narrator: Then he would eat breakfast with his wife and children.

Wife: Good morning, my husband! How did you sleep?

Rebbe: Fine, and . . .

Son: Good morning, Papa! Can I come with you to study today?

Rebbe: Yes, yes, my son, as long as . . .

Daughter: Papa, Papa, sit by me!

Rebbe: I always sit by you, my little Ruggeleh, today is no different! Such a family the Holy One has blessed me with. I am thankful.

Narrator: The Rebbe would finish his breakfast and walk briskly to the Bet Midrash, the House of Study, where students from far and wide would be waiting to study with him. For the Rebbe was known for his wise teachings.

Student 1: Rebbe, at last! I have traveled all week in order to study with you! I have many questions.

Rebbe: One at a time, please. I'll see what I can do.

Student 2: Rebbe, me first! This question is more important! Remember the argument David and I had yesterday, regarding the different opinions of Shammai and Hillel?

Rebbe: Let's think of it as more of a discussion than an argument.

Student 1: Hillel *always* has the right idea.

Student 2: I happen to think Shammai . . .

Narrator: Every morning the discussions would go on this way, with students debating important questions about right and wrong, good and evil, and so on and so on. Of course, when the Rebbe spoke, the students would quiet down and listen to the wise man's thoughts. This learning would go on until just past noon, when the Rebbe would say . . .

Rebbe: Students, we have fed our minds very well. Now what about our stomachs?

Students: Lunch!

(Students exit and the Rebbe walks back home.)

Wife: There you are! An hour late! Lunch is cold!

Rebbe: The discussion, it was going so . . .

Son: You should have been there! Tell them, Papa!

Rebbe: Well, you see, we . . .

Daughter: Papa, Papa, I learned a new song! Want to hear it?

Rebbe: Sure, how about after we . . .

Wife: Let's eat already, before it gets even colder.

Narrator: So the Rebbe and his family would eat lunch. No sooner would they have finished eating and bensching than a knock would come at the door.

Wife: I'll get it.

Woman: *(Entering.)* Please, Ma'am, I need to speak with the Rebbe.

Wife: I'm afraid he's just laid down to take a rest.

Woman: But, I've traveled such a long way . . .

Rebbe: Come in, come in. Maybe I can be of help to you. Let me hear your problems, and then I'll take my nap.

Woman: Thank you, Rebbe. You see, I heard that you were a wise man.

Narrator: She wasn't the only one. Yes, people would line up in front of the house to talk to the Rebbe. One after the other. So the Rebbe's nap would be postponed and postponed and postponed, until his wife would open up the door and say . . .

Wife: No more! Go home! It's time for our dinner! Come back tomorrow!

Narrator: And so the family would sit down to dinner.

Son: Papa, I want . . .

Daughter: Papa, I want . . .

Wife: My husband, I want . . .

Rebbe: Silence! Please! All of you! Let me eat in peace!

Wife: What's gotten into you?

Rebbe: Gotten into me? Nothing's gotten into me! Just that students come to study with me and all they do is argue! Do they ever really learn anything? And people come and want me to help them with their troubles? How do I know if I ever really help? And you, my dear wife, my precious son, my sweet daughter, am I really a good husband and father to you?

Wife: It's been a long day. Why don't you finish dinner and then take a walk.

Narrator: The Rebbe's wife always knew what he needed. So the Rebbe set out for a walk in the village. It was a dark evening and the streets were quiet.

Rebbe: How quiet it is, and peaceful. But dark. So dark. I can barely see my way.

Narrator: Just then, the Rebbe saw a light in the distance and he walked toward it.

Rebbe: Who else is out this time of night?

Narrator: The Rebbe looked up and saw a tall watchman.

Watchman: Hey! Who goes there? What do you want?

Rebbe: It is I, the Rebbe. I mean no harm. I was just taking a walk to quiet my mind.

Watchman: Oh, okay. It's just my job to stand here and make sure no one causes trouble.

Rebbe: I see. What is this place, that you are paid to stand here?

Watchman: This place? It's a mansion. There are many fancy, beautiful objects inside.

Rebbe: And who is it that you work for?

Watchman: I work for a rich man. He lives here — with his treasures.

Rebbe: Ah, yes. Well, nice to see you. I'll be on my way.

Narrator: As the Rebbe started to leave, the guard called out to him.

Watchman: Hey, Mr. Rebbe! Who is it that you work for?

Narrator: The Rebbe stopped and thought for a minute.

Rebbe: What a good question. I should pay you to ask me that question every night!

Narrator: And so the Rebbe walked home, a little faster now and with a lighter stride. He remembered now why all of his struggles were worthwhile, and when he reached his home his wife was waiting for him.

Wife: So. Did you enjoy your walk?

Rebbe: Did I enjoy my walk? Oh, my dear wife, you are wise to have sent me out. I realize now that even though some days life can be very frustrating, it is good to be alive. The Holy One gives us this beautiful world to do important work.

Wife: Yes, my husband, it is so. Now let us rest.

Rebbe: Let us rest.

(They exit.)

A Holy Place

(Grades 1-3)

Cast of Characters

Narrator
Ilana
Ronit
Husband
Daughter
Son
Toddler
Israelite 1
Israelite 2
King Solomon

Props

Two sacks for wheat
Ploughs, hoes, etc. (real or simply established with pantomime)

Costumes

Modern dress is fine. King Solomon may be dressed in more
finery than the other characters.

Narrator: Many, many years ago, in the land of milk and
honey, the place we now call Israel, there lived two sisters who
loved each other very much.

(Ilana and Ronit enter.)

Ilana: Ronit, I'm so happy we're sisters!

Ronit: Me, too, Ilana! You can always count on me . . . for
anything you need.

Ilana: Even when we grow up?

Ronit: Forever and ever!

Ilana: Me, too!

(They hug.)

Narrator: In fact, these sisters loved each other so much that they always wanted to live close by each other. So when they grew up, they decided to share a plot of land and grow wheat on it. In those days, there weren't any supermarkets or convenience stores.

Ronit: You can have the land from here all the way to there.

Ilana: Are you sure?

Ronit: Absolutely.

Ilana: All right. And you can take the land all the way from there to here. Deal?

Ronit: Deal!

(They shake hands.)

Narrator: Ronit and Ilana worked very nicely together, each taking good care of her share of land. As the years went on, Ronit got married *(Enter Husband.)* and had several children *(Enter Daughter, Son, and Toddler.)* while Ilana lived alone. Still the sisters lived and worked side by side.

(All characters actively work on planting wheat, hoeing, etc.)

Husband: This land is hard to plough. Maybe we should move somewhere else and find a better field.

Ronit: Move? How could we? You know I've made a pact to stay by my sister. Besides, I can't imagine living anywhere else. With our family here and Ilana beside us, this is the best place in the world.

Daughter: I'm tired of working in the field!

Son: Yeah! This is boring!

Toddler: Goo goo gah gee goo!

Ronit: What was that, honey?

Daughter: Baby said let's move somewhere easier to plough.

Husband: How did you know that?

Toddler: Gee gee gah goo goo!

Daughter: I know, baby. But they're just grown-ups. That's why they act so silly.

Ronit: Children, please! Go inside if you want, but I must stay here and plough. There's much work to be done on our part of the land.

Husband: I'll take the kids . . . see you soon.

Narrator: Just as Ronit's family was leaving the field, Ilana stopped working for a minute and began to think.

Ilana: Poor Ronit! She has so many mouths to feed! All of those children . . . and her husband . . . and herself! She has to work so hard. I, on the other hand, only have to worry about myself. And I always have plenty of wheat to eat. I make wheat bread and wheat biscuits and wheat-crust pizza and . . .

Narrator: Just as Ilana was thinking about all of her wheat treats, Ronit stopped working for a minute and looked across her field and began to think.

Ronit: Boy, am I lonely now without my husband and kids! And there is *so* much work for one person to do. Poor Ilana! She has to work alone all of the time, with no one to help her. Hmmm . . .

Narrator: Both Ronit and Ilana were deep in thought. Then, almost magically, an idea came to each of them at once.

Ronit: I know! I know! Tonight when everyone's asleep, I'll take a big sack of wheat over to Ilana! That will really help her! *(Pause.)* Why didn't I ever think of that before?

Ilana: I know! I know! Tonight when everyone's asleep, I'll take a big sack of wheat over to Ronit! That will really help her! *(Pause.)* Why didn't I ever think of that before?

Narrator: Both sisters went home to have dinner and to sleep.

Daughter: Nighty-night, Mom!

Ronit: Good night, honey. Sleep well.

Son: Night, Mom. And, uh, sorry about how I acted in the field. I know we all need to pitch in.

Ronit: It's okay. We all get tired of working. Sleep well!

Toddler: Gee gee gah gah goo goo gah.

Daughter: Baby says "I love you, Mommy."

Ronit: I love you all. Good night!

Husband: I'm ready to turn in, too. How about you?

Ronit: I'll . . . umm . . . be along soon. You go on ahead.

Narrator: As her family went to sleep, Ronit looked out her window. The moon was full and beautiful. Meanwhile . . .

Ilana: I'm so excited to leave this extra wheat for Ronit! I wonder if she's asleep yet. With all those kids, she must be worn out. I'll put out my light and be on my way.

Ronit: Ilana must be asleep by now. It's time for me to go.

Narrator: So Ronit set out with her sack of wheat for Ilana's house, and Ilana set out with her sack of wheat for Ronit's house.

(Ronit and Ilana walk on opposite sides of the stage.)

Narrator: Of course, they took the same path as always to each other's house.

(They meet center stage.)

Ilana: Ronit! What are you doing here? What's in that sack?

Ronit: Ilana! What are you doing here? What's in that sack?

Ilana: I wanted to share some of my wheat with you because I know you have so many mouths to feed . . .

Ronit: I wanted to share some of my wheat with you because I know you have to do all your work by yourself.

Ronit and Ilana: Ohh! You shouldn't have!

(They hug.)

Husband: *(Enters center stage.)* Ronit! What's going on! What were you doing in the fields so late at night?

Ronit: You'll never believe what just happened . . .

Narrator: Soon Ilana and Ronit and Ronit's whole family were wide awake and singing and dancing in the field!

Ilana: I always knew this was a holy place!

Narrator: People from far and wide heard their celebration.

Israelite 1: What's all this commotion in the middle of the night?

Israelite 2: Yeah, some of us work for a living and gotta get up in the morning!

Narrator: But as soon as the Israelites' heard about the sisters' love for one another, they stopped their complaining and joined in the celebration. News of the sisters' generosity traveled far and wide, reaching all the way to King Solomon himself.

King Solomon: *(Entering.)* You know, I've been waiting to find just the right spot to build Bayt HaMikdash, our Holy Temple. I needed to find a holy place — a place where people showed their love for each other, and in doing so, showed their love for God. You sisters have created just such a place — a holy place! This spot on Mt. Moriah is where we'll build Bayt HaMikdash!

Everyone: Yeah! Yahoo! Whoopee!

Israelite 1: Wow — I guess every place can be a holy place if we treat each other with love.

Israelite 2: If we think of the needs of others and not just of ourselves.

Husband: If we honor our sisters and brothers.

Son: If we help each other with our work.

Toddler: Gee gah goo.

Daughter: I agree. If we love each other as God loves us, every place will be holy.

The Land of Milk and Honey

●●●●●●●●●●●●●●●●●●●●●●●●●●●●●●●●●●●●

(Grades 4-6)

Characters

Narrator
Young Man
Father
Mother
Little Brother
Little Sister

Props

A cardboard tree
A traveling sack
A suitcase or trunk

Staging

This play is arranged in five short scenes that require only a
blank stage.

Scene 1

(Narrator stands just downstage of family.)

Narrator: A long, long time ago — before your Grandma was
born and before her Grandma was born and way before her
Grandma and her Grandma was born — there was a young boy
who wanted nothing more from life than to travel. This young
boy lived with his family in the land we used to call Babylon,
but all he ever heard about was . . .

Family: *(Together.)* . . . the land of milk and honey.

Narrator: Yes, the land of milk and honey. The place we now
call Israel. You see, every year at Passover, the young boy's
family, maybe just as your family today, would always say:

Family: Next year in Jerusalem!

Young Man: But I don't want to wait until next year! Why are we always saying, "Next year in Jerusalem"? We never get there, all we do is stay here. Stay, stay, stay, right here! I don't want to stay; I'm not a stay-er, I'm a go-er!

Narrator: Perhaps you mean a traveler.

Young Man: That's it, a traveler! So, I gotta do what a traveler's gotta do. I gotta travel!

Father: But my son, Jerusalem is many, many miles away.

Young Man: How many?

Father: Gee, I can't say.

Young Man: That's not so far. Besides, I'll ride our horse.

Father: But we don't have a horse.

Young Man: Okay. A boat must be leaving Babylon soon.

Father: Son, from here to Israel it's all desert. The great desert stretches out there as far as the eye can see. Sand and heat and snakes and scorpions — no water to found. Big sand, son. Big sand.

Young Man: All right, Dad, fine. I've saved up my allowance. I'll just buy a plane ticket and fly El Al to Jerusalem.

Narrator: Psssttt . . . I don't mean to interfere . . . but airplanes won't be invented for a millennium at least.

Young Man: *(Pacing back and forth.)* I don't have a horse. I can't take a boat. And airplanes haven't been invented yet. There must be some way, somehow, something that will get me to Jerusalem this year! Please, please God . . . I need a sign . . . anything . . . ouch, oh, boy, my foot just fell asleep.

Narrator: The best thing to do for a sleepy foot is just to walk on it.

Young Man: Walk on it. Walk on it. That's it . . . I'll walk to Jerusalem!

Scene 2

Narrator: So, like many travelers of the time, the young man prepared for his journey. As he imagined the sights and smells of the Holy Land, he packed a small sack with what he estimated to be enough provisions for the adventure at hand. The young man's mother had a different idea about what he should take along.

Mother: *(Carrying trunk-size suitcase.)* All right, son, if you must go, and you insist that you must, at least take along this little snack I prepared for you.

Young Man: But, Mom! How can I walk to Jerusalem carrying that thing?

Mother: But what if you get hungry?

Young Man: I've packed some things in my sack . . . and if I finish them, I'll . . . I'll . . .

Mother: You'll what?

Young Man: Stop at a supermarket?

Mother: The first one in Babylon is set to open exactly two thousand four hundred and seventy-seven years from now.

Young Man: Oh? Mother, I believe in this journey, and you always taught me that if you believe in yourself, the Holy One will help you to find a way. When the Israelites were wandering in the desert, wasn't there manna every morning when they awoke?

Mother: You are wise, my son. But at least take this pita and hummous. I don't think manna had much protein.

Scene 3

Narrator: And so the young man said farewell to his family and prepared to leave.

Father: You're sure you want to walk to Jerusalem?

Young Man: Absolutely — I've never been so sure of anything in my whole life.

Little Brother: Will you send me some milk and honey when you get there?

Little Sister: And some toys!

Mother: I don't think you should go all by yourself. Jerusalem is too far.

Young Man: If I shouldn't go, then why do we always say, "Next year in Jerusalem"?

Mother: We say it because . . .

Father: Because . . .

Mother: Just because.

Little Brother: I want to go, too!

Little Sister: Me, too! Me, too!

Little Brother: Me, three!

Little Sister: Me, four!

Young Man: Stop it! Stop, stop, all of you! And you wonder why I want to leave home.

Narrator: And with that, the young man picked up his sack and headed West. (*Cowboy music plays.*) No, not that West. West to Jerusalem. What? Yes, I know Jerusalem is in the Middle East, but from Babylon . . . well never mind. The important thing to know is that the young man began his travel by foot. He walked and walked in the hot sun. He stopped and rested and ate his food, and when the sun went down he slept. Then he awoke and walked again.

Scene 4

Young Man: Am I almost there yet?

Narrator: Not yet.

Young Man: Will I be there soon?

Narrator: How soon is soon?

Young Man: But I finished my food almost two days ago. I haven't had a drop of water all day. I don't think I can walk anymore. Could I at least have some shade?

Narrator: I think that could be arranged. (*Brings out a large tree center stage.*) Just as the young man was about to give up hope, he saw in the distance what looked like a giant tree.

Young Man: In the middle of the desert? It must be a miracle!

Narrator: What the young traveler didn't know was that the tree was a sign that he had almost reached the Holy Land, the land of milk and honey. A land where olive and date trees, myrtle trees, and palm trees grow, giving many gifts to the people. And because a tree must have water, a small stream ran beside this very special tree.

Young Man: Oooohhhh, tree, am I happy to see you! And apples! I love apples!

Narrator: And the traveler ate heartily.

Young Man: And water running beside you! Am I thirsty!

Narrator: And the traveler drank his fill.

Young Man: And shade! Boy, am I hot.

Narrator: And so the traveler slept soundly. And then he awoke.

Young Man: Boy, oh boy, am I refreshed. Now I can continue on to Jerusalem.

Narrator: But before going on, the traveler looked at the tree which had provided him with food and shade. And all at once the traveler became . . .

Young Man: Lonely! Boy am I lonely! Look at your branches, tree! You remind me of my father's big arms when he hugs me. And your trunk. You stand up so straight and tall like my mom. I miss you, Mom! *(He embraces the tree.)*

Narrator: And the traveler hugged the tree . . . uh . . . lovingly.

Young Man: You know, tree, I came on this journey because I couldn't wait to get away from my family. My sister and brother drive me crazy with their whining, and my mom and dad are always after me to do something or other. But I forgot about all the good stuff, all the stuff I love about them. I'm glad I made this trip, but I miss them. You must really be lonely way out here in the desert, all by yourself.

Narrator: So the young traveler thought long and hard about how he could cheer the tree up.

Young Man: You've given me so much, tree. I don't have anything to give back to you . . . except maybe a blessing.

Narrator: At last, the young man remembered that when one feels grateful for rest or shelter, or when one eats food, one says a blessing. But what kind of blessing would the young man offer to a tree that had everything it needed?

Young Man: Tree, you were so good to me. You saved my life. And so here is my blessing. May your seeds spread in this soil and grow a whole forest of trees just like you, so that you will never be lonely again.

(Young Man exits.)

Scene 5

Narrator: So, my friends, that is the end of our story. What? What about the young traveler? Well, he made it to Jerusalem that very day. And he liked it so much, he decided to stay and raise a family of his own in the land of milk and honey. Of course, he made many trips back and forth to Babylon to see his mother and father and his brother and sister. But the trip was never so hard as that first time. And so, if you ever go to that part of the world, and take that young man's long journey — just as you reach the Holy Land, look for a beautiful forest of trees. You will find fruit and water and shade there, and you will feel as if you're in the middle of a big, happy family. For with sincere blessings, a forest, like a family, can grow.

The Magic Tanach

●●●

(Grades 4-6)

Cast of Characters

Daniel
Esther
Tanach Man
Sarah
Miriam
Aaron
Caleb
Moses
Samuel
Isaiah
Jonah
Queen Esther

Costumes

Tanach Man can dress like Superman or Batman. Simple
pieces, such as a crown for Queen Esther, can be effective.

Props

The only prop necessary is the "Magic Tanach."

(Daniel and Esther are on stage.)

Esther: I can't wait for Purim! I'm going to win a prize for my
costume, I know it! I'll be the best Queen Esther!

Daniel: Just because your name is Esther doesn't mean you'll
win a prize.

Esther: Sure I will! Purim should be called "Esther Day."
People dress up like Queen Esther and we read in the Torah
about Queen Esther.

Daniel: No we don't!

Esther: Yes we do.

Daniel: We read about Queen Esther, but not in the Torah. We read the Megillah — it's a special scroll for Purim. It has the story of Esther written in it.

Esther: You mean I'm not in the Torah?

Daniel: 'Fraid not!

Esther: I don't believe you! Just because you're my older brother, you think you know everything. Prove it to me!

Daniel: Well, fine, Esther, I will! *(Pauses. Looks around.)* Uh, we don't have a Torah here. Or a Megillah.

Esther: Good excuse!

(A loud knock is heard.)

Tanach Man: *(From offstage.)* Yoo-hoo! Daniel! Esther! Open the door, would you?

Esther: Who is it?

Tanach Man: You don't know me, but I can happily answer your question!

Daniel: Yeah? About what?

Tanach Man: Your question about the Jewish Bible.

Esther: I'll open the door a crack . . .

(She does so and Tanach Man enters with gusto.)

Daniel: Who are you?

Tanach Man: Faster than a spinning dreidel! More powerful than a plate of horseradish! Able to solve deep problems in a single leap. I am . . . Tanach Man!

Esther and Daniel: Who?

Tanach Man: I am Tanach Man! I fly through the universe teaching children . . . and grown-ups . . . .and dogs and cats . . . and, well, anyone who will listen about the different parts of the Jewish Bible — the Tanach!

Esther and Daniel: The Tanach?

Tanach Man: That's right! Tanach is an acronym.

Esther: You mean a word created by combining the beginning letters of several words. Like MASH?

Daniel: Or MADD?

Tanach Man: Or Tanach. You see, the Torah is the first initial in Tanach. Do you kids know the different books in the Torah?

Daniel: Sure, there's Genesis, and Exodus, and . . . uh . . . some other ones.

Esther: Like the Book of Esther.

Tanach: Genesis, and Exodus, yes. Esther, no. That comes in a different part of the Jewish Bible. Well, lucky for us, it just so happens that I never fly around the world without my Magic Tanach. Let me reach in my bag . . . and here it is. Let's open to the Torah, the five books of Moses.

(Lights can go down. Sarah, Miriam, Aaron, Caleb, and Moses appear.)

Daniel*: Look at that! Who are you?

Esther: How did you get into our living room?

Tanach Man: What did you think — that I was a phony?

Sarah: Hello, I'm Sarah, I was sent to represent the Book of Genesis -- Beraysheet in Hebrew. It's the very first book in Torah. There you can read about my husband Abraham and me. Even before our story begins, you read about the creation of the world itself.

Miriam: And I'm Miriam, you may remember me from Exodus — Shemot — the second book. In Exodus, you can read about the Jewish people's journey from slavery in Egypt to freedom. Remember how I led the women in dancing after crossing the Sea?

Aaron: I'm Aaron, and I play a very important part in Leviticus — Vayikra — book three. In Leviticus, you read about the rituals of the priests and about holidays and moral laws, too.

Caleb: And I'm Caleb. You'll find me in the Book of Numbers — Bamidbar, which means "In the Desert." In Numbers, you read about the Israelites' years of wandering in the desert, hoping to make it to the Holy Land.

Moses: And I am Moses. You probably remember me from way back in Egypt. But I'm here to tell you about the Book of Deuteronomy — Devarim. Deuteronomy repeats many of the important laws . . . and it also tells the story of my death. I never did make it into the Promised Land.

(Lights go down, and Sarah, Miriam, Aaron, Caleb, and Moses exit.)

Esther: Miriam! Moses! All of you, come back!

Daniel: Hey . . . where'd they go?

Tanach Man: Sorry, kids . . . Tanach Man has much more to teach you!

Esther: But Sarah was standing right here in my living room. I didn't even get to talk with her.

Tanach Man: You'll have plenty of time to talk with her — and with all of them — once you understand the way the Tanach is set up. So let's continue. The "T" in Tanach was for . . .

Daniel: Torah!

Tanach Man: Very good! And the "N" stands for Nevi'im.

Esther: What's that?

Tanach Man: Nevi'im are the Prophets. I could tell you about them, but I would rather open my Magic Tanach . . .

(Lights out and Samuel, Isaiah, and Jonah appear on stage.)

Daniel: Whoa! Prophets!

Esther: Hmm. Still no Queen Esther. Well, who are you?

Samuel: I'm Samuel and I am a prophet of God. That means I'm a spokesperson for God's word. I was a leader of the Israelite people until my very old age. I appointed two kings of Israel.

Isaiah: And I am Isaiah, a prophet of righteousness. I speak God's words to a people grown rich and lazy. I remind people to live with good behavior.

Jonah: You probably remember me, too. My name is Jonah. I'm what you'd call a reluctant prophet. God called me to do a task, but I ran away. Eventually, I did the work God called me to do. Believe me, living in the belly of a big fish for more than three days is not my idea of a good time.

Esther: So you prophets teach people how to behave. Is that why you're in the Tanach?

Samuel: Absolutely!

Isaiah: We try our best!

Jonah: Even when it's hard, we share the word of the Holy One.

Tanach Man: And there you go. T is for Torah, N is for Nevi'im!

(Lights out, and Samuel, Isaiah, and Jonah exit.)

Daniel: Prophets are cool! Make them come back. I want to learn how *I* can be a prophet!

Tanach Man: Daniel, there will be plenty of time for you to get to know these prophets, but right now our journey must continue! The last letters in Tanach come from the word Ketuvim, which means Writings.

Esther: Writings! But I really just wanted to learn about Queen Esther!

Tanach man: I think that can be arranged.

(Lights out, and Queen Esther enters.)

Esther: Look! Could it be?

Tanach Man: Tell them why you're here, Esther.

Queen Esther: Well, that's easy. If you open the Tanach and are looking for my story, turn to Ketuvim. The Writings include any different kinds of books. Some are historical like the Book of Esther, and Ruth, Ezra, Nehemiah, and Chronicles I and II. Some writings are beautiful and poetic, like the Psalms, Song of Songs, and Lamentations. Some share deep thoughts, like Proverbs, Job, and Ecclesiastes. There is another book, too — the Book of Daniel.

Daniel: What? After all that, I discover I'm in Ketuvim? Cool!

Esther: We both are. That's super!

Queen Esther: So now you know the proper place to look for me. Come and find me!

(Lights out and Queen Esther exits.)

Esther: Wait! She's gone! Now that really wasn't fair.

Tanach Man: Not fair? My goodness, the Magic Tanach has shown you two how the Hebrew Bible is set up and where you can find what. What do you mean, not fair?

Daniel: She means it's not every day you meet Moses or Aaron or Queen Esther. You could have invited them to stay for lunch.

Tanach Man: Alas, that is where you're wrong, my friend! Every single day you can meet the characters in the Tanach. Every day you can learn about them and even have a conversation with them. It's not so magic, after all. All you need is a Tanach.

Esther: But you have a Magic Tanach!

(Tanach Man hands her the Tanach.)

Tanach Man: I'll let you in on a little secret, Esther. Every single Tanach is magical. Mine's not so special. In fact, keep it. I have plenty more. *(He pauses.)* Oh dear, me, the time. I must be going. Toodle-oo!

(Tanach Man exists out the front door.)

Daniel: Tanach Man — hey — where are you going?

Esther: Oh, let him go. He was kind of strange. Besides, we have his Tanach.

Daniel: What should we do with it?

Esther: Well, let's see if it really is magical. Let's start reading.

Daniel: First about Daniel, then about Esther.

Esther: No, first about Esther, then about Daniel.

(They exit, continuing to argue.)

In the Beginning

$\bullet$

(Grades 1-3)

(Note: This play is also appropriate for Shabbat.)

Cast of Characters

Narrator
Day 1
Day 2
Day 3
Day 4
Day 5
Day 6
Shabbat
Movement Ensemble

Production Notes

The movement aspect of this play makes it ideal for younger children. Scarves (for water, light, etc.), masks, and the like can be used to create an effect, or simple movements can be used.

(Narrator is alone on stage.)

Narrator: Just for a moment, close your eyes. See the darkness when no light seeps in. Now imagine way, way back, before God began to create the heaven and earth. It was darker than darker than dark. Look.

(Movement ensemble enters and twirls and whirls in a free form.)

Narrator: There was only dark, formless chaos. Chaos!

(Ensemble spins faster.)

Narrator: Fortunately, Adonai, our God, called out, "Let there be light!"

(Ensemble stops, stretches arms, and sways like sun rays.)

Narrator: And there was light. Much better. Whew, I can relax now. That darkness made me a little nervous.

(Day 1 enters.)

Day 1: Hey, wait a minute! Darkness isn't so bad. We sleep at night. We need night time to rest so we can enjoy the day.

Narrator: Hmmm. I guess you're right.

Day 1: Of course I'm right! So what God did was separate light from darkness. *(Divides ensemble in half. Half perform day movement, half night.)* God called the light day . . .

Narrator: And the darkness, I suppose, God called night.

Day 1: A good name sticks! So, we have evening and morning. The first day.

Narrator: So far, so good.

(Day 2 enters.)

Day 2: Have you ever looked out over the ocean as far as you could see, and it looked like the end of the ocean met the sky?

(Ensemble moves like waves.)

Day 2: On the second day, God separated the waters below *(Half the group gets on knees and continues to sway.)* from the waters above. *(Other half stands on tip-toe behind them and moves like clouds.)* Did you know that the sky is made of water?

Narrator: Are you sure about that? Clouds look more like cotton candy than water!

Day 2: It's water, all right. And there was evening, and morning. A second day.

(Day 3 enters.)

Day 3: No offense, Day 2, but a world made only of water wouldn't be so much fun. Suppose you didn't know how to swim?

Narrator and Day 2: Hmmm. You've got a point there.

Day 3: So on the third day, God made dry land appear.

Narrator: And I suppose God thought of some clever name for dry land, like "flijamagoobodybobbit"?

Day 3: Actually, God called the dry land "earth" (*Lower ensemble flattens out.*) and God called the water "seas." *(Other part continues as water.)*

Narrator: That works.

Day 3: But wait, there's more! With that deluxe model dry land called earth, you get vegetation! That's right, folks, seed bearing plants, like tomatoes, cucumbers, and avocados! And fruit trees — peach, plum, apple, fig — all on the very same day! *(Ensemble becomes plants and trees.)*

Narrator and Day 2: Whoa!

Day 3: That's right, folks! And there was evening! And there was morning! The third day.

(Day 4 enters.)

Day 4: Yeah, yeah, yeah. Fruit trees are okay. But how are you supposed to find the tree you want in the dark? So, God did some really spiffy stuff on the fourth day. God created the moon and stars to light up the night!

(Ensemble moves like fast burst of light.)

Day 3: That's not very light.

Day 4: I said the night! The moon and stars come out at night! When it's dark.

Day 1: Well, I'm getting cold. The moon and stars are pretty, but they don't do much to keep you warm.

Day 4: Presto-chango! Shabing-Shabang! Oh, and did I mention the sun? It's time for light! The sun is coming out! *(Ensemble moves like the sun, from east to west.)*

Narrator, Day 1, 2 and 3: Wow! Amazing! Fantastic!

Day 4: Now that's something! The sun keeps you warm, it brings light, and it puts on quite a show when it sets.

Day 2: Yes, but if a horizon hadn't been made on Day 2, you couldn't watch the beautiful sun disappear.

Day 3: And if there weren't fruit trees, made on Day 3, you couldn't pick an apple to munch while you watch the sun!

Narrator: Days, Days! Come on now, you're all special, in your own way.

Day 4: So we got the moon. We got the sun. It was evening, it was morning. The fourth day.

(Day 5 enters.)

Day 5: Okay, wait! My day is really, really, really cool! Okay, we have waters, right? What lives in the water? Fish, right? And every kind of really interesting sea creature! *(Ensemble becomes fish, sharks, etc.)* And if that's not cool enough, on that same day, God makes insects that creep and birds that fly!

Narrator: Like orangutans?

Day 5: Did you ever see an orangutan with wings? I'm talking about birds! *(Ensemble portray birds.)* Is that totally the best or what?

Day 4: Watch out. The birds might fly into the sun.

Day 5: So, it was evening. And morning. The fifth day.

(Day 6 enters.)

Day 6: Yes, yes, yes. I've been back stage waiting this entire time, watching your little show, and it has been very, very entertaining. But, don't you see? Day 6 is what really matters! On Day 6, God creates every kind of mammal! "Cattle, creeping things, and wild beasts of every kind!" *(Ensemble imitate various animals.)*

Narrator: Now we get your orangutans!

Day Six: And tigers and dogs and cheetahs and tree sloths and pandas — well, I could go on. But that wasn't all. Then God created human beings, in God's own image. God created male and female. *(Ensemble stands still.)* So you see why I'm so important.

Narrator: No, no, I don't.

Day 6: Don't you see? On the sixth day, human beings were made!

Narrator: Yes, I understand. And that *is* important. But, you see, Day 6, without God's first breath of light, and without the separation between water and sky, and well, without making dry earth and plants, and — of course — without sun and moon, and stars, and without fish and birds, and then without animals here to live beside us, I don't think men and women would be so important after all.

The Days: *(Together.)* Yeah! That's true! You're right! I never thought of that!

Narrator: We all make up creation together.

Day 6: Very well, but I happen to think Day 6 is just a teensy weensy bit more important!

Narrator: Shabbat! Quick! Please come out!

(Shabbat enters, dressed in a white robe. Ensemble stands, as if to greet a bride.)

Days: *(Together.)* Whoa! Who is this? What a beautiful day. She's like a bride. Looks like a queen to me.

Shabbat: I am the Seventh Day. On my day, God saw that heaven and earth were finished, and so God rested. God blessed the seventh day and declared it holy. On the seventh day, we do no work. On the seventh day, all the earth and sky, the darkness and light, water and land and plants, moon and stars, fish, birds, animals, and people, all are meant to be enjoyed. We rest, we thank God for our blessings, and we spend time with family.

Day 6: Seventh Day! You *are* really the most important. You are Shabbat.

Shabbat: On Shabbat, all of creation is holy and special. Every seventh day, the world is complete. On Shabbat, even God may rest.

Narrator: I could go for a nap about now.

(Ensemble, Days, and Narrator join hands and form a circle.)

Jonah's Job

(Grades 7-12)

(Note: This play is also appropriate for Yom Kippur.)

Cast of Characters

Narrator
Jonah
Voice of God
Sailor 1
Sailor 2
Sailor 3
Voice of Big Fish
Ninevite 1
Ninevite 2
Ninevite 3

Setting and Props

This play can be as theatrical as you choose. Sailors can hold a long blue sheet for a rocking effect or can rock their bodies. Jonah can sit alone on stage and act as if he were in the belly of a big fish, or the fish can be constructed out of papier-mâché or the like. Some sort of real or artificial plant is needed.

Production Notes

The Voice of God is always offstage, but the Voice of Big Fish can be on stage, depending on the staging.

Scene 1

Narrator: Hi, there. Have any of you ever heard the story of Jonah and the Big Fish? *(Takes audience responses.)* Wonderful. *(Narrator is suddenly struck with an attack of stage fright.)* Oh my goodness! I can't do this — I can't narrate a show. Uh, sorry audience — I gotta go! *(Runs offstage.)*

Voice of God: Narrator, you must return to the stage. You must tell these young people the story of Jonah's job.

Narrator: *(Entering reluctantly.)* How am I supposed to narrate a show when I have a terrible case of stage fright?

Voice of God: You must trust there was a reason you were picked for this position. Surely many people could narrate this show, but YOU were selected.

Narrator: All right, all right, I'll try.

Voice of God: Very well. Proceed.

Narrator: No, I think I'll proceed to say good-bye and go home . . . *(Starts to exit.)*

Jonah: *(Entering.)* Hey, hey, hey! The whole cast is waiting backstage! The play should have started five minutes ago. The actors are getting restless. *(Pause.)* Listen, we need you. Do you think you can try to change your attitude?

Narrator: You need me?

Jonah: Yes, we need a narrator. Otherwise the play won't make sense. And you are the person who was selected.

Narrator: You think I have a special ability at narrating?

Jonah: Yes, very likely. You see, when I was chosen to be a prophet — someone who speaks God's words to the people — I was afraid, too. Reluctant. I tried to run away.

Narrator: You did? Even a prophet tried to run away?

Jonah: Look, why don't we just get on with it and tell the story and then you'll see.

Narrator: Whew, do I feel better! If a *prophet* could run away, then . . .

Entire Cast: *(From backstage.)* Get on with it!

Narrator: Really, Jonah, I'm trying to do my very important job. After all, *I* was selected to be the narrator . . . so if you'll get backstage until I call you . . .

Jonah: Fine, fine.

Narrator: Way back when, before the Internet, before television, even before your own parents were born, there lived a man named Jonah. Jonah was called to be a prophet of the Holy One. *(Jonah enters.)*

Voice of God: Jonah, I've got a job for you. Go the city of Nineveh. The people there are wicked and they need to change. Tell them that for me.

Jonah: Nineveh. Yeah, that's the ticket. I'll hop the next boat to Nineveh . . . by way of Tarshish. *(Jonah stands as if hitchhiking.)*

Narrator: *(Confidentially, to audience.)* You must know that Tarshish is in the OPPOSITE direction from Nineveh.

(Sailors arrive.)

Sailor 1: Land Ho, mateys!

Sailor 2: Land Ho? We're not in Tarshish yet.

Sailor 1: Just yonder stands a man looking for a ship! We could use an extra hand around here!

Sailor 3: That's right! I'm sick of scrubbing the deck.

Sailor 2: And peeling potatoes.

Sailor 1: And hoisting those sails . . .

Jonah: *(Calling out to them.)* Hey, sailors! Where are you headed?

Sailor 3: Tarshish, good fellow!

Jonah: Just far enough from Nineveh! May I jump aboard?

Sailor 1: You got any experience sailing?

Jonah: Not much.

Sailor 2: Can you peel potatoes?

Jonah: Sure.

Sailor 3: Take him!

(Sailors anchor and Jonah hops aboard. In the next sequence, they show that they're on the water by rocking their bodies in a synchronized manner or using cardboard waves, etc.)

Narrator: So Jonah set sail. *(Pause.)* But God had not forgotten his instruction to Jonah. God was angry with Jonah because he ran away. And so God sent a great storm across the Sea.

Sailors and Jonah: *(Rocking.)* Woooaaahhhhh!

Sailor 1: I know! Everybody pray! I'll pray to the god of the water . . . maybe that'll help.

Sailor 2: I'll pray to the god of the wind . . . maybe that'll help.

Sailor 3: I'll pray to the god of potatoes . . . maybe that'll help.

Jonah: No, no — none of those things will help! There is no water god or wind god . . . and certainly no potato god! I believe in one God — the One who created the world and sustains us all . . . the one everlasting God!

Sailor 1: Hey . . . this guy's got connections.

Sailor 2: So do it already . . . pray to your big God!

Jonah: It's no use! God is angry at me, because I didn't listen to God's calling. There's no use in me trying to pray — the only way to save you all and to calm these wild waters is for you to throw me overboard.

Sailor 2: Into the water? You crazy?

Jonah: I disappointed the true God. I didn't accept my calling.

Sailor 2: Come on, buddy, the storm will pass.

Jonah: The sea won't get calm until you toss me in.

(Sailors look at each other, shrug their shoulders, and toss Jonah overboard. Jonah makes a falling motion and the sailors exit.)

Scene 2

(Jonah is curled up in a fetal position, center stage.)

Narrator: Actually, it was Jonah who didn't understand. Yes, God was angry. After all, God had given Jonah a job and Jonah refused to do it. But the one God is a God of justice and of mercy. So God took pity on Jonah and decided to save him. God sent a big fish to swallow him.

Jonah: Hey . . . have I drowned yet, or what? I'm still breathing! I'm not in the water. I'm in a cave of some sort . . . hey, how do I get out of here? HELP!!

Voice of Big Fish: A cave? Are you kidding? I've been insulted once or twice in my long life, but never like that! Me, a cave?

Jonah: What? Who's there?

Voice of Big Fish: You human beings are all alike! Here, your God saved you from drowning and all you want now is more help!

Jonah: What . . . who . . .

Voice of Big Fish: What, who do you think? Look around, Jonah. What do you see? A tongue? That's right. Teeth? Uh huh! A long, dark, throat and a big belly. I swallowed you up, baby — you're in the belly of a big fish!

Jonah: WHAT?

Voice of Big Fish: You heard me the first time — or are you pulling with me what you did with God. "Oh yeah . . . I'll go to Nineveh, by way of Tarshish . . ."

Jonah: I was going to go . . . I was just afraid . . . I mean I wasn't sure if . . . I . . . . Look, fish, let me out, please! I was wrong. I will do what God wants — I want to live!

Voice of Big Fish: It's not in my hands, Jonah — cause I'm only a huge fish. I don't have hands! *(Cracks up laughing.)* Seriously, this whole business is between you and the Almighty One. I suggest you pray.

Narrator: For three days and three nights, Jonah prayed. And God, the forgiving and just God, told the big fish to spit Jonah out on the shore.

Jonah: Don't take this as an insult, Creator of the Universe, but You have very strange ways of doing things sometimes.

Voice of God: Strange to people, perhaps. But that big fish understands me! Anyway, get to Nineveh and tell the people to change their ways. And this time don't go by way of Tarshish! Tell me, Jonah, do you think it's possible for people to change their ways?

Jonah: You know what they say — you can't teach an old dog new tricks.

Voice of God: Uh-huh. So the sea storm, the fish, that whole production . . . it hasn't changed you at all?

Jonah: Hmmm. Which way to Nineveh?

Narrator: So Jonah arrived in Nineveh and proclaimed to the people that they had 40 days to change their ways.

Ninevite 1: Forty days? To change our ways or perish? That's do-able.

Ninevite 2: God is very fair. We have been extremely wicked. And I always wondered what it would be like to be kind and righteous.

Ninevite 3: Me, too. Let's try it! Being good — that sounds like fun!

Jonah: That's all there is to it? I come and make this proclamation and you're ready to change just like that?

Ninevite 1: It *is* a proclamation from the Creator of the Universe, Jonah.

Ninevite 2: Yeah, what's with you? Have you been lost at sea or something?

Ninevite 3: Him a sailor? That guy probably can't even peel potatoes!

Narrator: So Jonah had done his job, and the people of Nineveh did change. They built a caring community in which people treated each other kindly and performed many good deeds. Of course, God forgave them. But Jonah was still a little angry over the whole thing. So he went to a quiet place east of the city and set up camp there.

Voice of God: Poor Jonah. He did his job, but he still doesn't get it. I'll send him a plant.

(Jonah sits alone on stage. A stagehand sets a plant beside him.)

Jonah: Hey! What a beautiful plant! You are a sweetie, growing here in the middle of nowhere! You'll provide me with shade . . . and we'll become friends. I've had it with human beings — *and* with fish! You and me, plant, we'll be okay together.

Narrator: But God had other plans. God wanted to teach Jonah a lesson. So God sent a wind which dried up the plant.

(Stagehand knocks plant over.)

Jonah: What? Hey, plant, my sweet, darling little plantie — wake up! Speak to me!

Voice of God: Jonah, you are very upset about the plant?

Jonah: You again! Yeah . . . why shouldn't I be . . . I loved this plant!

Voice of God: But you didn't work to create this plant. You did no gardening or watering even.

Jonah: So what?

Voice of God: So how do you think I feel? I didn't want the people of Nineveh to die. I created them, just as I created and I sustain you. I want human beings and all life to be strong, to be loving, to live well, and to forgive.

Jonah: I see . . . right . . . now I get it . . .

Narrator: And so this concludes Jonah's job, for in that instant, Jonah understood God's words — the very words that had led him on his journey. And so I ask each of you to think about times you have run away from important jobs, for maybe now . . .

Jonah: Hey, how about you, Narrator? You almost didn't narrate the show.

Narrator: That? My stage fright? Really, Jonah, that seems like years ago.

Jonah: So you like being a Narrator after all?

Narrator: Like? Jonah, let's face it — I was *chosen* to be a narrator!

Jonah: At least you didn't have to get swallowed by a large mammal to figure that out.

Narrator: Let's go backstage and compare notes, shall we?

Jonah: So long as we're on dry land!

(They exit.)

Reward without Measure

• •

(Grades 6-8)

Cast of Characters

Hannah
Mom
Malach
Woman
Older Woman
Student 1
Student 2
Ben
New Kid
Nice Kid
Grandpa
Bride
Groom
Jennifer
Sarah

Setting

Stage should be bare. Characters can enter and exit more easily without having to deal with set changes.

Props

Invitation
Beeper
Two pairs of sunglasses
Cane
Get well card
Lunch bags
Soup pot
Bowls
Ladle

Production Notes

Actors can easily play multiple parts. Simple costume pieces, such as a bathrobe for Grandpa, a veil for the bride, etc., will work nicely to establish character and are easy to change.

(Hannah and Mom are on stage.)

Mom: Oh, wow! Look what came in the mail today!

Hannah: What? Let me see!

Mom: It's Andrea's Bat Mitzvah invitation. It's really lovely.

Hannah: Let me read it! *(Takes invitation.)* On the fifteenth of Cheshvan, Andrea Lynn Zimmerman will become a Bat Mitzvah.

Mom: And I remember when your cousin was born! It seems like yesterday.

Hannah: Yesterday? It was almost 13 years ago. What does that mean — to become a Bat Mitzvah? I thought you *have* a Bat Mitzvah. *Becoming* one is a different thing.

Mom: Hannah, Bat Mitzvah means "Daughter of the Mitzvah." It means that Andrea is old enough to understand the mitzvot and observe them.

Hannah: You mean she has to do good deeds? Big deal. I'm nine, and I do plenty of good deeds.

Mom: It's more than that, Hannah. It's hard to explain. Mitzvot are commandments. We do them not because we feel like it, but because we should.

Hannah: Like brushing my teeth.

Mom: And flossing.

Hannah: Yeah, yeah. So Andrea will be a daughter of the mitzvot. What does she have to do exactly?

Mom: You know, Hannah, it's kind of complicated, and I'm already behind in all of my work. We can talk about it later.

Hannah: Oh sure, just let me die of curiosity.

Mom: Hannah, please! We'll talk about it later.

(Mom exits.)

Hannah: We learned in Religious School that there are 613 mitzvot. Andrea is really going to be busy.

(Malach enters.)

Malach: So you want to learn about mitzvot, and your Mom doesn't have time to talk right now. No problem. The Mitzvah Malach is at your command!

Hannah: Hey, how did you get in here? What do you want?

Malach: Is that a way to treat a messenger of The Holy One? Being the Mitzvah Malach sure is tough sometimes. At least Elijah gets a glass of wine when he drops in. But me — not so much as a glass of water!

Hannah: I'm sorry. Are you someone important?

Malach: I don't know about that, but I do have important things to teach — mitzvot, as a matter of fact.

Hannah: How did you know I wanted to learn about mitzvot?

Malach: Let's just say I've got connections. So let's get started. I never know when I'll get a call on my pager.

Hannah: Angels use pagers?

Malach: Well, a fax machine's too bulky to carry. Okay, mitzvot. It's true, there are 613 of them in the Torah. But for now, let's just look at a few. There's a section of Talmud that says, "These are the obligations without measure whose reward, too, is without measure." That means these mitzvot are so important that you can't even measure the goodness that doing them will bring you and others.

Hannah: Really? It's a lot of goodness?

Malach: You don't believe me?

Hannah: I didn't say that.

Malach: How about if you and I take a mitzvah journey? Put on these sunglasses. Hold my hand. Take a deep breath. WE'RE OFF!

Hannah: Hey, what's going on?

(Hannah and Malach spin around three times to indicate they've entered another realm.)

Malach: To honor father and mother — this is the first stop on our journey through the mitzvot without measure whose rewards are without measure.

(Woman and Older Woman with cane enter.)

Woman: Here, Mom, let me help you.

Older Woman: No, no, it's okay.

Woman: Mom, please, lean on me. I can help you walk.

Older Woman: It just seems like yesterday I was helping you learn to walk. Now look at me.

Woman: It's okay, Mom. You're doing just fine. Hold onto my hand, that's right. Here, let's go.

(They exit, Woman leading Older Woman.)

Hannah: That elderly lady really needed her daughter, just to walk.

Malach: And the daughter truly respected her mother.

Hannah: I wonder if my Mom will need me that way someday.

Malach: Maybe you will even be a mother who needs a daughter to help you.

Hannah: Honoring father and mother — that is a very important mitzvah.

Malach: Aha! Here comes mitzvah number two — to perform acts of love and kindness.

(Students 1 and 2 enter, dishing out bowls of oatmeal.)

Hannah: Hey, it's my Religious School class!

Student 1: I'm really glad we took on this mitzvah project of helping at the soup kitchen.

Student 2: But we have to get up so early to be here.

Student 1: But it's just once a week. Some people wake up hungry every single day.

Student 2: You're right. Helping out is a good thing.

(Students 1 and 2 exit.)

Hannah: I go to the soup kitchen, too. You mean I'm performing one of the most important mitzvot already?

Malach: All acts of love and kindness have reward without measure.

Hannah: Cool!

Malach: Next up, to welcome the stranger.

(New Kid and Nice Kid enter.)

Hannah: Hey! That's the new kid at my school. No one talks to him. He's from another school. He's really different.

New Kid: Lunch time. No big deal. I can sit alone . . . again.

Nice Kid: Hi, new kid. Do you want to sit at my table? I think we have some room.

New Kid: Me? Yeah, sure. That would be great!

Nice Kid: I always bring my lunch, too.

New Kid: Yeah, peanut butter is the only thing I eat for lunch.

Nice Kid: Really? Me, too.

New Kid: And I drink three juice boxes.

Nice kid: No kidding — so do I! Come on, let's go — I'm starving.

New Kid: Me, too!

(Nice Kid and New Kid exit.)

Malach: Is the new kid really so different from the other kids?

Hannah: No, he's not. I guess I could have been like the nice kid and welcomed him. It must be tough to be the new kid at a school.

Malach: Do unto others, as we say. Next mitzvah — visit the sick.

(Grandpa enters, holding get well card.)

Grandpa: *(Reading card.)* Dear Grandpa, I'm so sorry to hear you're not feeling well. I wish I could visit. Too bad we live so far away. But I'm thinking of you and I hope you'll feel better soon. Mom and Dad said we'll come visit during our next school vacation. Love, Hannah. Oh, that sweet Hannah. This card really made my day — it's almost as good as a visit. I can read it again and again.

(Grandpa exits.)

Hannah: Wow. I had no idea Grandpa liked my card so much.

Malach: When someone is sick, a visit or a card or a phone call can really cheer them up. It's no fun to feel lonely when you're not feeling well.

Hannah: We did get to see Grandpa, and he's doing much better now.

Malach: Good, good. Let's move on to my favorite mitzvah — to rejoice with bride and groom.

(Bride, Groom, and bridal party enter, dance a brief "Hora," and exit. Hannah and Malach join in.)

Hannah: I'm out of breath! What a fun mitzvah.

Malach: Absolutely. Judaism teaches us that celebrating is just as important a mitzvah as consoling the bereaved.

Hannah: What does that mean?

Malach: Comforting someone who's mourning. When someone dies, we support the family who lost a loved one. We go to the funeral and sit shivah with them. We listen when they need to cry or share memories about their loved one.

Hannah: I know, shivah lasts for seven days. I went to shivah at my friend Shoshana's house when her Grandma died.

Malach: So you know about that mitzvah. Good. I sort of sneaked that one in, didn't I? What's next? Ah yes — to pray with sincerity.

Hannah: You don't have to show me that one! I understand it. When you talk to God, really talk, it doesn't matter if you're in synagogue or at home or wherever. Sometimes I pray when I'm up in my tree house.

Malach: You're catching on, Hannah. You don't need me anymore.

Hannah: Come on — there must be more!

Malach: Oh, we can't forget this mitzvah — to make peace where there is strife.

(Jennifer and Sarah enter.)

Jennifer: I can't believe you told my secret! You were my friend, but now I never want to talk to you again!

Sarah: I didn't tell, I promise. Come on, Jennifer.

Jennifer: I don't know why I was ever your friend to begin with.

Sarah: Oh, really! Well, it wasn't me who wanted to be friends with you!

Hannah: Jennifer, Sarah! Why are you guys fighting? Come on, we're all good friends. This is ridiculous.

Jennifer: Friends don't tell secrets.

Sarah: But I didn't. I'm telling the truth.

Hannah: Come on, let's talk this out. Good friends can always talk stuff out. I know Sarah wouldn't tell a secret. And, Jennifer, I know you must really be upset to get angry this way.

Jennifer: Yeah, I don't know what I'm saying. I did tell my secret to three other people who might have told. Sorry, Sarah, let's talk this out, okay?

Sarah: Okay!

(Jennifer and Sarah exit.)

Malach: Well, well, well! Way to jump in there, Hannah. You've clearly learned the mitzvot whose rewards are without measure. I can take you back home now . . . and go answer my next page.

Hannah: Wait, Malach — one more question. My cousin Andrea is becoming a Bat Mitzvah, a daughter of the commandments. I know she's been studying her Torah portion like crazy. So what does Torah study have to do with all this?

Malach: Put on your sunglasses.

Hannah: Huh?

Malach: Put them on. *(Hannah does so.)* Take a deep breath. Grab my hand and we will quickly and quietly leave this mitzvot journey so you can return to life and start practicing these mitzvot.

Hannah: But my question! What does Torah study have to do with . . .

Malach: Take off!

(As they spin three times, Malach speaks.)

Malach: . . . and the study of Torah is equal to them all, because it leads to them all!

(They "land," and Malach nonchalantly exits. Mom enters.)

Mom: Hannah, I was thinking . . . the mitzvot are more important than my work. Let's talk about them now.

Hannah: Can't, Mom, I have a lot to do. Study, good deeds, visit the sick, honor my mother . . .

Mom: Say, you already seem to know a lot about mitzvot. *(Pause.)* Hannah, where did you get those sunglasses?

Hannah: Let's just say . . . a little angel gave them to me.

(They hug and exit.)

Rabbi Akiva and the Tree of Life

(Grades 4-6)

Cast of Characters

Narrator
Rabbi Akiva
Sheep
Rachel
Student 1
Student 2

Costumes

Simple pieces may be used to give this play a historical flavor, such as sandals for Akiva and the students, etc. The "sheep" can wear a furry coat or just a sign around its neck that says "Sheep."

Production Notes

This play can be useful when teaching history or the essence of Torah.

(Narrator enters, glancing at watch.)

Narrator: Shalom, Chaverim! So sorry I am late. I have just come from studying Torah, and when I study Torah, I lose all track of time! Do any of you lose track of time when you're doing something that you love? Yes? Well, for me, nothing is better than reading the stories in the Torah, because each time I do, I learn something new. Oh my, here I am talking, and all the while you are waiting, waiting so patiently for our play to begin. I'm sorry, but when I talk about how I study Torah, I just forget about everything else! *(Looks at watch.)* Okay. We shall begin with our presentation about Rabbi Akiva and the Tree of Life.

(Akiva and Sheep enter.)

Akiva: You know, I have a good life as a shepherd. I go out to the field with you sheep every day, and I get to sit and think. I think about all kinds of ideas, I think about the sun and the moon, the stars and the earth. I think of how the earth was created. Though sometimes I wish there was someone I could talk to . . . besides you sheep.

Sheep: Baa-aaa.

Akiva: What would it be like to be around other people, thinking about the world, about happiness and sadness, life and death?

Sheep: Baaa-aahh.

Akiva: You know, Sheep, I mostly like to think about God — the Creator of the entire universe.

Sheep: Well, in that case, you should leave the field already and go study Torah.

Akiva: What? You can talk?

Sheep: You pick up certain things when you hang around human beings a lot. So either I can talk, or you've gone crazy talking to sheep all day. Anyway, I'm telling you what to do — go study Torah. Haven't you ever heard, the Torah is a Tree of Life? It contains everything — all the stuff you mentioned — how the world was formed, good and evil, and it most definitely talks about God.

Akiva: But how do you know all this?

Sheep: I may walk on four legs and say "baa," but I wasn't born yesterday.

Akiva: But this Torah you're talking about, how *do* you study it?

Sheep: It's no great mystery. You sit around with a group of people who also want to learn, and you read the Torah and talk about it.

Akiva: Read! But I can't read!

Sheep: So, you'll have to learn.

Akiva: But I'm 40 years old. The other students would laugh at me.

Sheep: Suit yourself. Stay out here with us sheep all day when the Tree of Life is there waiting for you.

Akiva: Well, I want to study Torah, but on the other hand, learning to read, that'll be hard. Do you think I can do it, Sheep?

Sheep: Baaaa-aah!

(They exit.)

Narrator: So, Akiva put much thought into the idea of learning to read and study Torah. Later that night, he decided to discuss the issue with his wife, Rachel.

(Rachel and Akiva enter.)

Akiva: So. Did you think about anything exciting today?

Rachel: Exciting? Hmmm. I was thinking we should have lamb chops for dinner tomorrow.

Akiva: Oh. That's nice.

Rachel: Is something wrong?

Akiva: No, no . . . well, yes. Rachel, I have a crazy idea. I don't know what you'll think about this.

Rachel: Akiva, I love you. You can tell me anything.

Akiva: What if I said I want to give up being a shepherd and go learn to read so that I can study Torah?

Rachel: I would say that I know you are a wise man. I believe you can do anything you set your mind to.

Akiva: But I will have to leave our home and study far away.

Rachel: I'll miss you very much, but this may be your destiny.

Akiva: I'll miss you, too, and I'll return as soon as I can.

Rachel: I think you should set out tomorrow.

(*Rachel and Akiva exit.*)

Narrator: Despite his fear, Akiva set out for the academy. There many students were talking excitedly about the stories in the Torah.

(*Rabbi, Student 1, and Student 2 enter. Akiva enters from the other side.*)

Student 1: Why did it take God six days to make the world?

Student 2: Could you do it any faster?

Rabbi: Perhaps the question is: why did God rest on the seventh day?

Akiva: Well, everyone needs to rest sometimes, and after doing something so incredible as creating all of time and space, even The Holy One may have wanted to rest.

Rabbi: Ah-hah! I see we have a real Torah scholar, a learned man, in our presence! Come in, come in, sit down, we're just in the middle of a discussion.

Akiva: Actually, I've never studied Torah before in my life.

Student 1: What? Never studied?

Akiva: To be completely honest, I don't even know how to read.

Student 2: Can't read? What sort of dummy are you?

Akiva: I'm just a poor shepherd. I came from very far away. I left my wife and home so that I could start to study the Tree of Life.

Rabbi: My friend, though you may not know how to read, and may never have seen a Torah, it is quite clear that you know much about the Tree of Life. Sit down, have some tea, and let's study. We'll begin at the beginning, with the Alef-Bet.

(All exit.)

Narrator: And so Akiva learned the Alef-Bet, and from there, spent many hours studying the Tree of Life. Akiva became known as a great Rabbi, and people from all over came to study with him. So you see, it is never too late to start your studies — or to do anything you really want to do. As for me, I want to learn all I can from the Torah, so I must get going.

(Sheep enters.)

Sheep: Excuse me!

Narrator: Yes. Who are you and what in the world do you want?

Sheep: I'm the Sheep . . . remember? From the beginning of this play. Did you leave your brain in the dressing room?

Narrator: You startled me! Sheep can't talk.

Sheep: Either I'm talking or you've been standing under bright lights too long. Anyway, I heard you were going to study Torah.

And I'm kind of curious about this whole Tree of Life thing. Mind if I tag along?

Narrator: But you're a sheep.

Sheep: And Akiva was 40 years old and couldn't read.

Narrator: You're right! Come along, then. Uh . . . um . . . what shall I call you?

Sheep: Reb Asheepa sounds good to me!

(They exit.)

The Secret World
of the Alef-Bet
● ●

(Grades 4-6)

Characters

All the Hebrew letters, from Alef to Tav

Costumes

Use T-shirts and fabric markers or poster board and string for
the various characters. Simple costume pieces such as hats,
beards, glasses, etc., can help to distinguish between them.

Production Notes

This play can be useful for both younger students first learning
the Alef-Bet, as well as older students dealing with more
complex use of the Hebrew language.

If there are not enough students for each part, assign each
actor multiple roles.

(All "letters" stand in alphabetical order in a single file line.)

Tav: Okay, guys and gals, Morah's finally gone. You can
stretch!

(Letters stretch, sigh, shake their limbs, etc.)

Dalet: I know we're doing an important thing by posing at the
front of the class, but I get tired of standing in one place all
day.

Lamed: You and me both. And hearing her say my name —
Lamed — almost halfway through the Alef-Bet. That really
lights my fire. I mean, Lamed begins many important words
you know.

Mem: Name one.

Lamed: Okay. How about *"lilah,"* as in night? As in *lilah tov.* Like right now it's *lilah.* The students are home and we can move around.

Bet: The students are home arranging us letters into words. If they didn't remember our order, they could hardly even begin to spell. I don't mind standing in order for them.

Nun: Yeah, Bet, that's 'cause you come at the beginning! For me, Nun, I don't come till after my friends Lamed and Mem.

Bet: Order is order. Learn some patience!

Gimel: That's right. Obviously, whoever created the Alef-Bet knew what was right!

Koof: I have an issue I'd like to share. I don't mean to be a party pooper, but I do have a real problem, and it's with you, Caf. I've tried my best to ignore it, day after day, but I just can't take it any longer . . .

Caf: Why, Koof, what is it?

Koof: I'm Koof, I come at the end of the Alef-Bet and I don't complain about that. I like my sound, I begin many important words like "kadosh," which means holy.

Caf: So what's wrong then?

Koof: People always confuse me with you!

Caf: Well, we do both have the "k" sound after all.

Koof: But students get so frustrated. Just today, four Koofs were circled in red ink, because they should have been Cafs!

Samech: You think that's bad? I'm Samech, the "s" sound. Well, lo and behold, in Hebrew, we have two "s" sounds!

Sin: And you don't hear me getting upset over a little confusion, Samech. Sometimes you feel like a Samech, sometimes a Sin.

Shin: Yeah, and Sin and I have figured a great way around our own little confusion!

Samech: What's that?

Shin: Well, as you can see, Sin and I look exactly alike . . .

Sin: Except for our head dot.

Shin: And since I'm a "sh" sound and my dot's on the right . . .

Sin: We just say "she's always right!"

Shin: Or, it's no sin to be a lefty!

(Shin and Sin laugh hysterically while others look at them.)

Tav: Great, great, great. You know, I — Tav — sound like another letter myself.

Tet: That's me, Tet! Letter number ten, right between Chet and Yod!

Tav: And that makes you better, I suppose?

Tet: I like my place, that's all.

Tav: Well, I'm getting mighty sick of being at the very end of the Alef-Bet. It's simply not fair! Every single time the students say the Alef-Bet, I have to wait until Morah calls Koof, then Resh, then Shin, then Sin, and then she always says — "and last, but not least" — Tav!

Resh: I like being at the end. It's a good place for Resh.

Tzadi: Look, Tav, I'm toward the end of the Alef-Bet, too. But Tzadi is such a unique letter, students always remember me, so I don't care where I go.

Zayin: Snob.

Tzadi: What did you call me, Zayin?

Zayin: Tzadi, I called you a snob! Snob!

Tzadi: Sticks and stones . . . oh forget it. I know I'm special. I have a "tz" sound and there is nothing like that in English! Zayin, you sound just like a boring old "z."

Zayin: Hebrew has lots of unique letters, Tzadi, but you don't hear them bragging!

Tzadi: Like who?

Chet: (*Makes throat clearing sound.*) Achem. The sound one must enunciate in order to make a "Chet" is rather unlike anything in the English language.

Chaf: Good point, Chet.

Chet: Achhemm. Do take that into consideration, Tzadi.

Dalet: I'm not so unique, I suppose. I sound just like a "d."

Lamed: Oh, Dalet, you're lovely! Think of all the great words you start!

Dalet: Like what?

Mem: How about "Dayaynu"?

Dalet: That's right — Dayaynu! It would have been enough!

Nun: We're forgetting some very important, very unique letters.

Resh: Yeah? Who else?

Nun: The ones who never speak for themselves! The ones who are always quiet and just listen! Alef and Ayin!

All letters except Alef and Ayin: Ohhh. Ahhh.

Nun: *(Alef and Ayin step forward. Nun points at them as if selling a product.)* That's right, folks. Silent letters. In formal speech terms, Alef is a glottal stop and Ayin is a pharyngela voiced stop. But for us, just remember that Alef and Ayin are not difficult to pronounce at all. They simply take a vowel to give them sound. Now, that's what I call unique!

Tav: Sure, Alef doesn't mind being silent! Alef is first! And Ayin has that neat shape! But for those of us down here at the end of the letter list, and especially for me, Tav, it's just not fair! Either we devise a new order or I quit!

Vav: You know, I — Vav — haven't said much today, and neither have the letters Hay or Yod. But I've been listening to you complaining, Tav, and I need to bring something to your attention.

Tav: What's that?

Vav: Well, you see, we're only letters after all. Letters are nothing on their own — it's only together that they can build words.

Hay: And then as words, they can build sentences, and paragraphs, and books!

Yod: Letters express ideas, thoughts in people's heads.

Vav: But some ideas are so important, so true, that mere letters can not even explain them.

Tav: Ha! Maybe some letters can't, but I can explain anything!

Vav: Hay and Yod, let's show Tav what I mean.

Hay: Will someone please become another "Hay" for purpose of a demonstration?

Samech: Sure, I will. (*Puts on Hay shirt or sign.*)

Vav: Okay, let's get in order now.

(*They spell out Yod Hay Vav Hay*)

All letters: Yod Hay Vav Hay.

Hay: Together, our letters express the idea of God, The Holy One. But we can not *be* God's name, as hard we try. To spell out God's exact name is something no letter can do.

Chet: Even a Chet, with my special gargling sound, can't be God's name.

Tav: I suppose you're right. We are just letters after all.

Bet: Hey, guys, look at the time! The Morah will be coming back soon, and the students, too. Get in line!

Resh: Time flies when you're making words.

(*All letters form a line.*)

Shin: Are you still mad about being at the end, Tav?

Tav: There are more important things about a letter than just its order in the Alef-Bet. Really, Shin, when will you learn?

Climb the Tzedakah Ladder

(Grades 1-3)

Cast of Characters

Morah
Student 1
Student 2
Student 3
First Rung
Second Rung
Third Rung
Fourth Rung
Fifth Rung
Sixth Rung
Seventh Rung
Eighth Rung

Props

Desks or chairs
A ladder

Production Notes

An actual ladder is a good visual device, or use a large painted poster of a ladder. "Rungs" should enter and exit at their turn, perhaps standing just to the side of the ladder itself.

(Morah and students sit in a classroom set-up.)

Morah: Okay, Talmidim, who remembers what "tzedakah" means?

Students: *(All together)* JUSTICE!

Morah: That's right! Very good! Tzedakah translates into *justice.* And what are some ways we can do tzedakah?

Students: *(All together.)* I don't know!

Morah: Hmmm. Well, in that case, we have a lot to learn today. Fortunately, we have some help. You see, Moses Maimonides, a Jewish teacher who lived way back in the twelfth century, came up with a sort of tzedakah ladder that helps us learn how to create a just world.

Student 1: A ladder? What does that have to do with tzedakah?

Student 2: Does justice have something to do with painting houses?

Student 3: Maybe that's how you do tzedakah. You get up on a ladder and then . . .

Morah: Hold your horses! This isn't just any old ladder — this is an "Eight Degrees of Tzedakah" ladder we're talking about. *(She brings out ladder.)* Rung Number 1, what can you tell us about tzedakah?

First Rung: Not much. I'm at the bottom of the tzedakah ladder, and there's a good reason why. I don't really want to be on the ladder . . . I just know I should be on the ladder and so I am. But I wish I weren't!

Student 1: But what do you do, First Rung?

First Rung: When we talk about giving tzedakah, we mean giving money or volunteering time to make the world a more just and fair place for everybody. So I give my share . . . well, not quite my share. And usually someone has to ask me first.

Student 2: That rung doesn't sound very just to me!

Morah: On to the Second Rung . . .

Second Rung: Now when *I* give time or money, I do so with all of my heart! I really really really really do! It's just . . . well . . . I know I could give more . . . I mean, I guess I don't give my fair share, exactly.

Student 3: But if we want to create a fair world, doesn't everybody have to give his or her fair share?

Morah: Exactly! Rung Number 3, come on down.

Third Rung: Now me, I give exactly what I should, no matter what the cause! Save the dolphins, save the whales, save the dolphins from the whales! You name it, I'll give. Just ask me!

Morah: Aha — therein lies the problem? What do you think, students?

Student 1: You have to *ask* that rung to give!

Morah: And let's compare this with the Fourth Rung . . .

Fourth Rung: When I see a problem in the world, I want to fix it! You don't have to ask me — I give tzedakah whenever I see a need.

Student 2: What could be wrong with that? How could doing tzedakah be better than that?

Morah: Calling Fifth Rung!

Fifth Rung: When I give tzedakah, I don't even want to know where it's going! I just want to give. Of course, if the recipient knows who I am and wants to thank me later . . . well, that's just fine with me.

Student 3: I think that rung likes recognition.

Morah: I think you're right. Sixth Rung!

Sixth Rung: I'm happy to give whenever, wherever I can. And I don't want recognition. Just list me as "anonymous."

Student 1: Anonymous! Now that's humble! How can you get better than that?

Morah: Wait and see. Seventh Rung!

Seventh Rung: When I give tzedakah, I find a way to do it so that I don't even know *where* my tzedakah money is going. That way, I can't possibly know the people my tzedakah money is helping . . . and I can't feel superior to them. Believe it or not, some people (*Looks pointedly at Fifth Rung.*) give money and then want recognition or lots of thanks. And some people see who they give to and then think, "Hey, at least I'm not that poor soul." I don't think that's bringing more justice into the world.

Student 2: Now that rung is really on track! You give . . . without knowing where you're giving. And the person who benefits from your tzedakah doesn't even know it's from you.

Morah: But wait, we have one more rung to learn about . . .

Eigth Rung: In Maimonides' ladder of tzedakah, I am the highest rung. Did you ever hear the saying, "Give a man a fish and he'll eat for a day . . . teach him to fish, and he'll eat for a lifetime"?

Student 3: No — never heard that before.

Eighth Rung: Well, you see, instead of just giving money or time to a cause, I help another person learn to support himself or herself. I teach someone a skill, help someone find a job, or discover some way that person can be independent so he or she doesn't need to receive tzedakah.

Morah: And, in fact, there are times in our lives when any one of us might need help from someone else. And Judaism teaches us that there's no shame in needing help. The only shame is in being selfish and not helping.

Student 1: We have learned a lot about justice today.

Student 2: You know, I think I knew more about justice than I thought I did.

Student 3: It's pretty simple. Do good deeds just for the sake of it. Help people learn how to make their lives better. And don't do it because *you* want people to think you're a big shot or something. All in all, I'd say tzedakah sounds pretty smart.

Morah: Remember, we've got Maimonides to thank for this wonderful ladder. Look, time's up. Class is over. I'll put the ladder away.

Student 1: Uh, pardon me, Morah, but could I borrow that ladder for tonight? My Dad and I are painting our living room.

The Crown of a Good Name

(Grades 7-12)

Characters

Jacob
Sally
Mom
Historian
Rabbi
Great Grandpa Jake
Great Grandma Sarah
Government official
Jew 1
Jew 2
Jew 3
Jew 4
Maimonides

Costumes

When characters from an earlier time (such as Maimonides or the older relatives) appear, a simple hat, turban, or shawl may be used to indicate that era.

Staging

Jacob, Sally, and Mom don't interact directly with the other characters. They are softly frozen when those characters appear.

(Jacob appears alone on stage, acting as if he were performing a monologue in a theater.)

Jacob: What is in a name? Would not a rose smell as sweet?

Sally: *(Entering.)* Hey, Jacob, who are you talking to?

145

Jacob: Huh? What? Nothing . . . I mean, no one.

Mom: (*Entering.*) "What's in a name? Would not a rose smell just as sweet . . ." I forget the rest. *Romeo and Juliet.*

Jacob: Mom, you know Shakespeare?

Mom: Not personally, but I did take my share of literature courses way back in the olden days before you two were born.

Jacob: I get extra credit in English if I can recite this monologue in class tomorrow.

Sally: You, reciting Shakespeare? You were too nervous to try out for the school play!

Mom: Shakespeare's not so hard. First you have to figure out what he's talking about. What do you think — what *is* in a name?

Sally: What do you mean?

Mom: Well, what's Shakespeare asking? Does a name really mean anything? Would you still be Sally if we called you something else? Would you be Jacob if we called you "Hey You"?

Sally: Well, I'm not just Sally. Don't forget my Hebrew name is Sarah Leah. That's important because I'm named after Great Grandma Sally and your cousin Len.

Mom: That's right.

Jacob: Why do Jews do that? Name kids after relatives who have died?

Mom: It's an Ashkenazic custom. Hundreds of years ago, Jews started naming their children after relatives who had died.

Sally: We learned about that in Hebrew School. Some say the custom goes all the way back to the days when the First

Temple was destroyed in 586 B.C.E. and the Jews fled to Babylon.

Jacob: Maybe they started naming new babies after people who died in the Holy Land so they would remember them, even though they were living far away.

Mom: Aha! So, a name can be a connection.

Sally: Why did you name me after Great Grandma Sarah? What was so special about her?

Mom: I wish you could have met her, Sal. She was one of a kind.

(Great Grandma Sarah enters and stands downstage, somewhat away from the others.)

Great Grandma Sarah: I wasn't so special, I just tried my best to be a good person and be humble before God. Times were tough for me, I left the old country when I was just 16 and came to New York all by myself. I stayed with a cousin and worked as a seamstress, sometimes 12 hours a day. Then, one day, I was in a pharmacy, and the young man behind the counter was very kind. That was your Great Grandfather Jake! Oy, did I fall in love . . .

Mom: Great Grandma Sarah was hardworking and kind. She was generous and full of love for everyone. Those are qualities we wanted to pass on to you, Sal.

Sally: Wow. That's a lot to live up to!

Jacob: Well then, why didn't you name her Sarah if she's named for Great Grandma Sarah? What's with Sally?

Sally: Yeah!

Mom: Many Jewish families give kids two names — a Hebrew name and an English name. Some people use the first letter of the Hebrew name to begin the secular name. Besides, I thought you'd like the name Sally.

Sally: Well, yeah, I do. I just thought maybe it wasn't authentic or something.

Mom: Well, let's look in a Jewish encyclopedia and see what we find.

Historian: *(Enters and stands in "special" spot.)* For many centuries, in many different cultures, Jewish children have often been given a secular name to be used for common purposes and a Hebrew name for religious purposes. For instance, the Hebrew name Baruch, which means "blessed," became *Benedict* (or "blessed" in Latin). Even in Eastern Europe, where Yiddish was the spoken language, a child's name might be hyphenated in Hebrew and Yiddish, such as the common Dov-Baer, both of which mean "bear."

Jacob: That's kind of neat. But who would want to be named bear?

Sally: It could be worse. Like elephant. Or donkey.

Mom: Funny, you mention that, Sal. You know, it's only recently that Jews have had formal last names . . . and not everyone ended up with the most attractive choice.

Jacob: No last names? How would you tell one Jacob from another?

Mom: Back to the encyclopedia.

Maimonides: *(Enters and stands downstage.)* I have no "formal" last name as you do today, but everyone knows who I am — Moses Maimonides, a scholar, a physician, a writer, one of the best known commentators on the Mishnah to date! You see, in fourteenth century Spain where I lived, a person was known as so and so, son of so and so. I am Moses, son of Maimon. The "ides" ending is a Greek suffix meaning "son of."

I am also known as Moses ben Maimon, for in Hebrew "ben" means "son."

Sally: That seems to work okay. So what happened? What changed?

(Government Official and Jews 1, 2, 3, and 4 enter and stand downstage.)

Government Official: Hear ye, Hear ye! As of this date in the year 1787, all people residing in Austria must have a last name! That includes all Jews!

Jew 1: A last name? Well, my family members are Kohanim, descendants of priests, so I'll be David Kohane!

Government Official: Make it Cohen and we're in business.

Jew 2: My husband is a goldsmith, so we will be the Goldschmidt family!

Government Official: Goldschmidt, got it. Next!

Jew 3: I can't think of anything! My mind's blank! Well, my favorite color is Roth . . .

Government Official: Roth it is. *(To audience.)* That's German for red.

Mom: Not all government agents were so nice. Sometimes they demanded a bribe in order to give you a good name.

Jew 4: I'd like Greenberg because I live by such a beautiful green mountain.

Government Official: Greenberg, everyone wants Greenberg! That'll cost you, buddy, or otherwise you end up with Eselkopf!

Jew 4: But that means donkey's head!

Government Official: Green mountain or donkey's head — you decide!

Sally: We lucked out with Goldberg!

Mom: So, what do you think, Jacob? Is there something to a name after all?

Jacob: What about my name, Mom? I know I'm named for Great Grandpa Jake.

(Great Grandpa Jake enters.)

Jake: I would have been proud to know you, Jacob. Your mother may not know this, but even though I was a pharmacist, my great love was literature. In the back of the store, I kept Shakespeare, Keats, Shelly . . . and, of course, my Tanach. I always loved to read . . . How I loved to learn!

Mom: Your Great Grandfather was very learned, Jacob. He was very modest, but he could recite just about every Shakespeare sonnet by heart. That came back to me when I heard you before.

Jacob: Yeah, but, before your Grandfather, the name Jacob came from the Torah. Why was *that* Jacob — Isaac and Rebekah's second son — called Jacob?

Mom: Let's take our translation of the Torah.

Biblical Jacob: *(Enters and stands downstage.)* It says in Genesis 25:26, "Then his brother emerged, holding on to the heel of Esau; so they named him Jacob." Ya'akov, Jacob, comes from "aykev," which means heel. In the Torah, names in and of themselves tell you about the person. Even as a baby, I held onto Esau's heel because I already had the desire to take my older twin's birthright.

Sally: Jacob was really confused. Just because you're not the oldest doesn't mean you're not important.

Mom: Well, think about the rest of his story, Sal. Jacob needed to learn that lesson.

Biblical Jacob: Believe me, I paid a price for taking Esau's birthright. I had to come face to face and reconcile with him later. He wasn't so happy with me, you know. But that wasn't my hardest encounter ever. You see, before I was to meet Esau, I was camped out overnight. And a man came to me and challenged me to a wrestling match, which lasted until dawn.

Jacob: A wrestling match? Wow!

Biblical Jacob: I don't know if it was actually a man or an angel of God. I wrestled until he knew he couldn't win. Finally, he stopped challenging me, and I knew I had triumphed. He asked for my name and I said, "Jacob." Then he changed my name to Israel, which means "one who wrestles with God."

Jacob: Now, that's cool! From now on, call me Israel.

Mom: We can all be Israel when we live up to life's challenges.

Jacob: Like learning this Shakespeare monologue?

Mom: That's right.

Jacob: What's in a name?

Sally: I think names really do matter.

Mom: At a funeral, I once heard a Rabbi say something very wise.

Rabbi: *(Entering.)* As the great Rabbi Simeon said, "There are three crowns: a spiritual crown, a royal crown, and the crown of Torah. But the crown of a good name is greater than all three." Whatever our name is, it is our work in life to bring honor to that name.

Jacob: Maybe if I learn this monologue, I'll even see my name in lights someday. That would have made Great Grandpa Jake proud.

Sally: I try to be hardworking like Great Grandma Sarah, but I know I could try harder.

Mom: I'm very proud of both of you. You wear the crown of a good name.

Jacob: Maybe if I wrestle with this "What is a name" thing, I could even take on a new name.

Mom: Like what?

Jacob: Shakespeare. Shakespeare Goldberg.

Sally: Sweet!

Mah Tovu

●●●●●●●●●●●●●●●●●●●●●●●●●●●●●●●●●●●

(Grades 4-6)

Characters

Morah
Student 1
Student 2
Student 3
Balaam

Props

Several desks or chairs
A blackboard and anything else that will establish a classroom setting
A school bell

(Students sit at desks and Morah stands.)

Morah: Boker Tov, Talmidim! *(Pause.)* Can anyone — please — tell me what I just said?

Student 3: Good morning, students!

Morah: Yofi, yofi, yofi! Okay, b'seder. Today we'll be studying the prayer "Mah Tovu." Let's start with those two words. Who remembers what Mah means?

Student 2: Oh, I know! Hello, good-bye, or peace.

Student 1: How come she always gets everything right?!

Morah: Let me take a deep breath. Inhale, exhale. No, Talmidim, the word for "hello, good-bye, or peace" isn't Mah. Hello, good-bye, or peace is . . . is . . . is . . . *(No answer from the students.)* Hello. Good-bye. *(Getting angry.)* Or PEACE IS . . .

Balaam: *(Entering.)* Shalom!

Morah: Finally! Who said that?

Balaam: Shalom, Morah Beckwith. It was I, Balaam.

Student 3: Who's that?

Student 2: I heard there was a new kid coming to Hebrew school, but my Mom said he'd be in Moreh Shapiro's class.

Student 1: He looks a little old for fifth grade!

Student 2: He must have flunked a bunch of times.

Student 3: You mean you have to stay in Hebrew school until you pass? From now on, I'm doing my homework!

Balaam: Talmidim, Morah Beckwith, Shalom. I'm sorry to interrupt your class, but when I heard you were studying "Mah Tovu" today, I couldn't help myself. I just couldn't stay away.

Morah: Who are you? Are you registered in the office? Do you have a hall pass?

Balaam: I'm sorry, Morah Beckwith, I do not. My name is Balaam. Perhaps you remember reading about me in the Book of Numbers. I was sent by the King of Moab to curse the Jewish people, but when I came upon their camp and saw how beautiful and peaceful it was there, I blessed them instead.

Student 2: Are you the real Balaam or just some Balaam look-alike?

Balaam: I'll tell you what, students. Let me share with you the story of "Mah Tovu," and then you can decide if I am the real Balaam. Is that all right, Morah Beckwith?

Morah: I really wish you had a hall pass, but the way this class is going, it can't get much worse.

Balaam: Talmidim, the words Mah Tovu mean "how good." You remember the word "tov," as in Boker Tov?

Students: *(Together.)* Good morning!

Balaam: Nachon! So you see, I said those words "Mah Tovu" when I came upon the Israelites dwelling together in the desert. Keep in mind that I was known as a sorcerer, and King Balak of Moab sent me on a special mission to curse the Israelites.

Student Three: Why did he want to curse them? What did they ever do to him?

Balaam: Well, that's the point of the whole story! There was no reason to curse them, no reason to hate them. I was just going along, doing my job as I was told. The Israelites were a people different from us, with different ways. As far as I can see, that's why Balak wanted me to curse them.

Student 1: But that's not right, not to like someone just because they're different from you.

Student 2: Yeah, a lot of my friends from public school are of religions different from mine — and we like each other just fine.

Student 3: Yeah, and I have friends at my school from a lot of different countries. It's neat to go over to their houses for different holidays.

Balaam: Yes, yes, but *why* do you enjoy their holidays?

Student 2: Well, all of their family and friends come and people celebrate and have fun together.

Balaam: And what about the reverse? Do you have friends come to your house to celebrate the Jewish holidays?

Student 1: My friend Sally comes over for Shabbat all the time. She loves it!

Balaam: Have you ever asked her why?

Student 1: Not really. It's just a special time for my family. We're all together, we eat my Grandma's homemade challah, and we sing our favorite songs.

Balaam: Yes, that very feeling — the love of family and friends celebrating and worshiping together in peace — that's what I saw when I looked upon the tents of the Israelites. That's why I couldn't curse them. Instead I said, "How good your tents are, O' Jacob! How fine your dwelling places, Israel!"

Student 2: Well, you know, I have my own tent. My boy scout troop goes camping all the time. And it's a good place.

Balaam: That's right. Any place you go . . . whether it's a tent or your house . . .

Morah: Or your school . . .

Student 3: Or your friend's house . . .

Student 2: Or your synagogue . . .

Student 1: Or a stadium . . . if you get tickets . . .

Balaam: Yes, anywhere you go can hold the love of the Israelites' tents. Anywhere you honor The Holy One and honor each other becomes a holy place.

(Bell rings.)

Morah: I'm afraid time is up for our Hebrew lesson today, Talmidim. And we only got to the first words of "Mah Tovu."

Balaam: Which means?

156

Students: *(Together.)* How good!

Balaam: Yofi, yofi, yofi, as Morah Beckwith says! Sorry we didn't cover more, Morah, but I should be on my way back to my own tent. My donkey is waiting outside and is probably pretty anxious to go.

Morah: Yofi! Well, Talmidim, what do we say to Mr. Balaam for stopping by?

Students: *(Together.)* Todah Rabbah!

Morah: Wait. I didn't teach you that. How did you know that?

Balaam: You know the old saying, Morah Beckwith. When the mouth is ready, the words appear! Shalom, Chaverim!

(Balaam exits.)

Morah and Students: Shalom, Balaam!

(Morah and students softly sing "Mah Tovu" as they exit.)

NOTES

NOTES

NOTES

NOTES

NOTES